The Physician's Practical Guide to Insurance

The Physician's Practical Guide to Insurance

ARNOLD GEIER

The Macmillan Company *New York*

A DIVISION OF THE CROWELL-COLLIER PUBLISHING COMPANY

First printing, June 1962

Library of Congress catalog card number: 62–11917

The Macmillan Company, New York
Brett-Macmillan Ltd., Galt, Ontario

Printed in the United States of America

DESIGNED BY RON FARBER

This book is dedicated to
William VanRiper Cadmus
and
Allan A. Steinitz
who introduced me to a fascinating career.

Preface

Dr. Harry Benson listened attentively. John Kiler, his lifelong friend, paused to sip his iced drink. John had done well for himself.

"Being the general manager of the store has meant a lot to me, Harry," he continued. "It has made me a nice living and has given me time off to enjoy the family."

I have a nice living too, Dr. Benson mused silently, *but not much time for the family.*

"Not only that, but it has provided me with security all these years. Do you realize, Harry, that the survivor benefits of my social security represented about $60,000 to me while the kids were young?"

Yes, I know that. I had to buy insurance to give my family the same security.

"When I retire, social security will give me a lifetime income. I figured it out, Harry. I would have had to invest about $38,000 at 4 per cent after taxes to equal what I'll receive."

And I had to pay a pretty heavy premium for that retirement policy.

"Down at the store we have a fine group insurance program; hospitalization, major medical, life, and disability income. And it costs me practically nothing!"

But I pay plenty for these coverages.

"Our profit-sharing plan has built me a pretty substantial retirement fund."

I have a profit-sharing plan too. My grocer is just one of many who share in my profits.

"Remember when I told you about the stock options I had in the store? Well, I used them and the stock is worth plenty today."

John really made out alright. As a physician, I have had to accumulate and pay for these benefits myself. I only hope I made the right moves!

Are you making the right moves?

This book is designed to guide you through the oft-complicated maze of the insurance industry and its products. It is not a technical thesis. It deals with the practical application of insurance to your particular needs and desires. It warns you of pitfalls in planning. It explains the meanings of clauses and provisions which are often buried in legal or technical jargon. It saves you the time you would have to spend with several insurance advisors in order to get impartial and complete information.

The physician cannot take advantage of social security, company group insurance, pension plans, stock options, and many other valuable benefits available to business executives. The physician's financial planning depends mainly on himself. This book will assist you in utilizing insurance to the greatest advantage in such planning.

An intelligently planned insurance program translates intangible concepts such as love, devotion, and concern into tangibles such as home, food, education, necessities, luxuries, and into money when it is most needed. It is often the only way for a physician to obtain a measure of security.

The author hopes this book will bring you closer to that goal.

Contents

List of Tables

The Physician's Practical Guide to Insurance

1. *The Birth of Life Insurance*

"You have to crawl before you can walk," goes the popular saying.

Life insurance groped through a black maze of you'll-die-if-you-own-it type of superstition, ignorance, bungling, misinformation, and trial and error for several centuries.

The exact origin of life insurance is lost in antiquity. Guesses pertaining to the probability of life and death were recorded in the laws of the Romans. Ancient burial and funeral societies tried to provide funds for widows and orphans through membership dues. Benevolent societies, guilds, and fraternities also tried to create benefit funds for the families of their members.

Very few of these attempts, however, were based on scientific methods and sound principles. No recorded experience was available on which to base predictions of longevity.

In 1661, John Graunt, a London haberdasher interested in the science of probabilities, made a major contribution to the birth of the insurance industry by publishing a table prepared from the mortality registers of London. This traced the history of deaths of a large group over a period of decades. In fact, he prepared the earliest known scientific attempt at a mortality table, a statistical study of the "journey through life" of a large group of men all starting this journey at the same time.

Countless important studies along these lines followed during the next century, including a most significant one by Dr. Edmund Halley of Halley Comet fame.

Several companies attempted thereafter, but failed, to build a life insurance business. It was not until enough scientific calculation and experience had been compiled that life insurance was ready to be considered on a solid enough foundation to give birth to a modern industry.

London, in 1752, saw the birth of the life insurance industry. The Society for Equitable Assurance of Lives and Survivorship, still flourishing today, was the offspring.

The first American life insurance company was founded in 1759 by the Presbyterian Synod of Philadelphia to benefit the families of its clergy. The Presbyterian Ministers Fund, as the company is known today, is still operating with distinction.

The Mutual Life Insurance Company of New York and the New England Life Insurance Company of Boston, both in operation today, represent the first establishments of modern life insurance companies in the United States. Both issued their first policies in 1843.

As more companies came into existence in the United States, new mortality tables, based on American rather than British experience, were devised and adopted. The life insurance industry was on the way to phenomenal success.

Many inequities, however, existed in the policies of that day. If a premium were not paid on the day it was due, the policyholder would lose his protection and, usually, his investment. Even if small cash values were granted upon surrender of the policy, they had to be claimed within a short time. Statements in the applications for insurance were considered warranties, which permitted a company to void a contract if any word on the application were proven not literally true. Most of today's standard clauses were unknown.

These inequities and abuses caused the state of New York to form the Armstrong Committee in 1905. Based on its investigation and recommendation, new laws were enacted in New York State and in other interested states. These laws established definite protection and guarantees for the policyholder as we have them today. New York State still maintains one of the most watchful and strict insurance departments in the United States.

The insurance commissioner of each state exercises tight control over all companies operating within his boundaries. His department may, and does, audit a company's books periodically to ascertain its continued solvency. All changes, additions, or modifications of policies must have his approval before they can be effective. He literally holds the power of financial life and death of the insurance companies and their agents within his jurisdiction.

The birth of the insurance industry was a tedious and difficult one. The "stumbling baby," however, has grown to a strapping, energetic young man. Centuries of glorious service yct lie before him.

2. *Why Life Insurance?*

Civilized families have one thing in common—they spend money. One may spend more than another, but all spend. Money, then, is the universal tool that provides us with food, clothing, housing, educational and professional opportunities, luxury, leisure activity, travel, hobbies, cultural endeavors, industry, business, and almost everything else short of life, faith, love, and patriotism. In our society, money must be spent in order that man may exist.

An income represents spendable dollars. That which produces the income is the goose that lays the golden eggs. It is either you at work or your money at work.

Life insurance concerns itself mostly with the family whose income is dependent upon "you at work." Your life has a tangible economic value to your family, your community, and your society.

Were you to go on an extended trip, you would most certainly leave enough money in the checking account to permit your wife to carry on the family's daily life until your return. Does your family deserve less if your trip, unfortunately, becomes a permanent one?

No one can replace a husband and father. But life insurance can replace his economic value to his family. It can serve as a living memorial of love, tenderness, affection, and concern. It keeps the family unit together by enabling the mother of your children to stay at home and raise them as you want them raised. Without it, you may be forcing her to become the breadwinner, leaving the children to their own devices. It educates orphans, grants dignity and independence to widows, and prevents disaster from falling upon an innocent household.

The physician has one major capital asset: his life. His extensive and expensive training, his devotion and skill, his industrious service are all wiped out at death. The family is bankrupt. Is it not logical, then, for the physician to insure the value of his earnings over a normal life span, just as surely as he insures the replacement values of his car and home? Is it not also reasonable for him to consider the gradual depreciation of his physical capacity for work as he gets older and to prepare himself financially for the day when this capacity becomes extinct and he can no longer work? A life insurance policy is a legal contract which helps bring plans to completion and turns goals into realities. In a sense, it buys time. The vast majority of men require decades to accumulate a substantial estate from surplus earnings. An early death leaves the dream unrealized. Life insurance creates an immediate estate for him who was not granted enough time to accomplish this by himself.

The primary purpose of life insurance is the replacement of your economic worth for the continued protection and well-being of your loved ones. At the same time, however, it becomes an instrument of thrift to compensate you when physical depreciation forces you to slow down or cease working altogether. It provides you with income for life. It serves as unequalled collateral for business opportunities and stands ready with funds during illness or emergencies.

Life insurance dollars build homes, factories, hotels, hospitals, and businesses. They create millions of jobs, finance research, and substantially help to keep the national and local economy moving. They educate children, keep families fed and healthy, make widows and old people secure financially as well as psychologically. A life insurance policy creates confidence, trust, understanding, and faith. It is a successful endeavor of thinking men to spread the risk of untimely interruption of their productive lives among themselves. Alone, their resources and time cannot guarantee the creation of the needed estates. Together, with the aid of science and the law of averages, they can create certainty out of the uncertainty of living which all of us face.

3. *Insurance Companies*

They Manage Your Money

"Always buy from stock companies," one insurance man advises.

"Doctor, you will come out much better in a mutual," another confides.

"What's the difference?" you ask.

Four types of companies issue policies in the United States. They are stock, mutual, fraternal, and combination companies.

STOCK COMPANIES

A stock company is one which is owned by stockholders. It operates as any corporate business. The stockholders assume responsibility for proper management. They also assume the risk of losses and enjoy the rewards of profits. Most stock companies issue policies which are nonparticipating (do not pay dividends) and which guarantee that your premium will remain the same as long as you own your contract. Any unusual losses must be absorbed by the stockholders. To minimize this risk, stock companies are often more conservative in accepting other than first-class risks. Some stock companies do issue a few participating (dividend-paying) policies for special package plans or special risks.

MUTUAL COMPANIES

A mutual company is legally owned by the policyholders. All monies belong to, and are managed for the benefit of, the policyholders. Each is entitled to a vote at the annual directors' meeting and is, at least in theory if not in actuality, empowered to condone, condemn, replace, or rehire the management.

Mutual companies, which insure by far the greatest number of people in the United States, issue participating (dividend-paying) policies. They charge a higher premium than is actually necessary. At the end of the year, they calculate the benefits paid out, the proportionate funds necessary for future benefits to be paid, the expenses of operating the company, and deduct these sums from the premium and investment income received. Whatever is left over, they apportion according to amount, type, and age of policy. They then return a sum to the policyholder as a dividend, which is actually a refund of money not used. Mutual companies do not guarantee any dividends since everything depends on a favorable mortality experience (less than the expected number of claims paid during the year), a good return on company investments, and sound management to keep operating expenses to a minimum.

Most major American companies are mutuals.

FRATERNAL SOCIETIES

Fraternal societies usually operate similarly to a mutual company. Their policyholders, called members, have banded together because they have something in common. This may be religion, nationality, occupation, or other interests. Thus, a fraternal insurance society is a branch of a small or large fraternal organization; one which holds meetings, elects officers, and is active in the community. Members of the Knights of Columbus may obtain insurance from the Knights of Columbus Fraternal Insurance Society. Members of Polish background may obtain insurance from the Polish-American Alliance. Labor Zionist Jews may be insured with the Farband, a fraternal society dedicated to Labor Zionism. There are some fraternal benefit societies which do not have a religious, regional, or national background, but are organized solely for insurance purposes.

Most fraternals have special benefits in their certificates (the name used instead of policies) which appeal to its members. Some operate old-age homes for destitute members, others make visiting-nurse services available.

A few fraternals include matters of ethics or cannon peculiar to their own organizations in their certificates. Some are so organized as to permit assessment to each member, either by direct contribution or through a temporary lowering of cash values, in the event the society faces sudden financial difficulty.

It is interesting to note that some of our major insurors had their origins as fraternal benefit societies. Today, there are few large fraternals still significant in the over-all picture of insurance.

COMBINATION COMPANIES

Combination companies are stock companies which incorporate some of the features of mutual companies. They may issue both participating and nonparticipating policies. They may actually be operating two companies under one group and one management. Because of this arrangement, combination companies often make it possible for their agents to work most effectively by giving them the opportunity to combine participating and nonparticipating coverages into one program.

In the states of Massachusetts, New York, and Connecticut, mutual savings banks are authorized to establish insurance departments which sell term, permanent life, and endowment policies over-the-counter. These policies are similar to regular commercial types, except that they limit selection of various payment settlements and do not issue any disability or accidental death benefits. No agents are employed and no commissions are paid. Although his premium is lower, the buyer of savings bank insurance deprives himself of the benefits of a professional insurance counselor.

4. *Insurance Agents*

Is Yours a Good Agent?

The M.D. after your name certifies to the public that you have met the necessary requirements in terms of education, training, and skill in order to qualify in the healing of the ill. The state adds its recognition by issuing a license to practice. Experience, advanced studies, specialization, personality, and many other factors add to your prestige as a doctor in the eyes of the public and your colleagues.

An insurance agent, however, can obtain a license without undergoing very much training. The companies try to be selective before committing themselves to the necessary financial backing in order to launch an agent's career. Their first objective is to prepare him for his license examination. He can devote two or three weeks to intensive study and pass the examination easily. This examination tests his general knowledge of insurance terminology, ethics, rules, laws, and other basic subjects. Since he is not permitted to sell insurance without a license, he has no practical experience whatever when he embarks on his career. But, as far as the world is concerned, he is legally qualified to help the public in financial planning.

Fortunately, the physician will rarely deal with the neophyte of the industry. The new agent usually solicits his family, friends, and neighbors first. By the time he has finished this campaign, he is either ready to leave the insurance business or he has gained invaluable experience. His agency manager has probably held numerous conferences with him to help him gain an insight into the complexities that arise in many instances.

After several years of intensive study, formal courses, and the proverbial school of hard knocks, the agent becomes a counselor in the true sense.

Then, you are ready to place your confidence in him. Then, too, he will have enough confidence in himself to approach you. You may deal with several agents, but once you have found an individual who obviously has the necessary knowledge, training, and experience, and who never shirks from performing an unreimbursed service cheerfully, stick with him. This does not mean that you should close your mind to anyone else. On the contrary, if one of your colleagues recommends that you meet an insurance counselor of particular quality, by all means meet him. You will either learn something new and improve your insurance program, or you will have your faith in your own man confirmed.

Beware of the agent who can make a diagnosis of all your financial problems after a few minutes of friendly conversation.

Beware of the agent who urges you to drop an equity-building life insurance policy. He is more interested in writing you a new policy and earning the first year's commission than he is in your welfare. Only rarly is the recommendation to drop a permanent life insurance policy an honest one. Most existing life policies can be changed within the original company without loss to you.

Beware of the agent who is so indoctrinated by one company that he refuses to recognize the fact that other companies may have certain policies that can be of more value to you. Every agent, except an independent agent or broker who can place business in any company of his choice, will first try to place your policy in his own company. After all, he may receive a greater commission, he may have quotas to meet for favorable financing arrangements, or there may be a company production contest. The good agent, however, knows his company's weaknesses and will not hesitate to broker your business with another company if this is to your advantage.

Beware of the agent who is not a man of his word. If a promise is made to have certain information available at a certain date, to provide you with certain services, and this promise is not kept, you have reasonable cause to doubt the agent's over-all integrity.

Beware of the agent who constantly criticizes other companies and agents. This does not include the conscientious advisor who points out shortcomings in a contract you are considering.

Beware of the agent who mails policies instead of delivering them in person and going over each provision.

The insurance industry has made great progress in educating its men. Most companies offer elementary and advanced courses. The Life Underwriters Training Council holds classes all over the United States to teach the fundamentals of all phases of personal insurance. The College of Life Underwriters offers advanced courses leading to the highly respected designation of Chartered Life Underwriter. Thousands of agents are presently engaged in these lengthy courses. They are sincerely interested in being well equipped to help you in your financial planning.

You must remember that a good agent is interested in guiding you as best he can. Therefore, extend to him the same courtesy and confidence you would to your accountant, attorney, or colleague. Give him the full information he seeks, talk freely, and don't hesitate to ask questions. If, due to an emergency, you cannot keep an appointment, call him. His time is valuable, too. Don't let him sit in your waiting room unnecessarily. The loyalty and effort you will receive in return will amaze you.

5. *Your Application*

Now That You Have Signed on the Dotted Line

"Thank you for your confidence, Doctor," the agent says, as he gathers up the application, "I'll put this through right away."

What actually happens to your application from that moment?

The agent returns to his agency's office, goes over the papers to make sure they are complete and accurate, and gives them to the agency's secretary. She copies the basic information such as name, address, date of birth, and beneficiary, on a form supplied by a reporting company such as Retail Credit Company or Hooper Holmes. The original of this form is sent to the reporting company, where an inspector uses that information to contact one of your colleagues or neighbors to corroborate these facts. He tactfully tries to uncover information dealing with habits, character, reputation, and any other matters that may be of interest to the insurance company in their evaluation of you as a risk.

The application is mailed by the agency's secretary to the home office of the company.

Clerks at the home office prepare data sheets which show that the application, medical examination form, investigation report, and other necessary papers have been received. The file moves to another department which sends inquiries to the company's private sources of information, requesting recorded facts about you, if any. If you have ever been rejected for insurance or have had a policy issued on a modified basis (other than originally applied for), these sources will report this to the company. Then the file arrives at the underwriting department. Highly trained underwriters review all aspects pertaining to you; physical, moral, financial, and so on, and recommend approval, modification of your requested coverage, or rejection of the application. The medical director, a physician, lends his knowledge to approve modification or rejection of the risk.

Very often, additional information is needed by the underwriter or medical director before a final determination can be made. Clerks are then instructed to inform the agent of the information required or, what is most common, a request for specific information is sent to the physician who has treated you in the past. After this information is received and the application has been approved, the file is sent to the policy issue division. The exact premium is calculated, a policy number is assigned to you, the policy is typed, photostatic records are made, the whole file is checked and rechecked, and the policy is mailed to your local agency. There, the agent checks it again, calls you for an appointment, and delivers and goes over with you the policy for which you have applied.

Some policies are issued within 10 to 15 days. Many times, however, there may be time-consuming complications. For example, the investigation, which includes a check at previous residences, may require reports from several cities; the doctor from whom information is sought may be too busy to give it immediate attention; your medical examination, which should be completed soon after you apply for a policy, sometimes takes place long after you have signed the application; your agent may not have obtained exact addresses or other vital information; the method of settlement you request in your policy may necessitate work by the legal department.

The home office is anxious to get your case approved as quickly as possible. Every delay is an expense in time, effort, and money.

To assure yourself of prompt issue, always give your agent complete information. Be especially careful to state the full names and addresses of physicians who have treated you. Arrange to be examined as soon as possible.

Do not be surprised if a courteous inspector makes discreet inquiries about you. It is standard procedure with all insurance companies to hire a reporting company for that purpose.

You should also remember that one of *your* colleagues or former patients may have his application held up while an insurance company awaits a report from *you*. Send these reports back as soon as possible. Without them, a tragedy may occur and be on your conscience.

6. *Insurance Premiums*

How Your Premium Is Calculated

Have you not often wondered how the insurance companies arrive at the premium you must pay for your particular policy?

The calculation of premiums is almost a science. It requires a highly trained actuary, supplied with facts on investments, sales, and related matters, to arrive at a premium figure.

If you and nine colleagues decide to create a fund with which to pay the widow of any one in your group $1,000 on the day he dies, you would have to invest only $100 each. The fund would be ready, and the $1,000 would be available at a moment's notice. Dr. Benson dies, and the money is delivered to Mrs. Benson. Now there are only nine men left. Each must now put in $111.11 in order to create a fund again totaling $1,000. Another colleague dies. His widow receives the money.

Like the proverbial little Indians, there now remain only eight of you. Again the required contribution goes up, this time to $125 each. It is becoming increasingly prohibitive to be a surviving member of the group. The older your colleagues get, the less practical the system appears. Eventually, this method fails because at a time in life when the survivors inch closer to death, the cost to them becomes so prohibitive and the relative benefits so small that it is no longer practical to continue this program.

The life insurance industry recognized the total unsuitability of such a system. It devised a mathematical formula enabling it to fix a premium so as to anticipate the future cost of insurance. The premium accurately reflects all present and future risks and obligations that must be met as the policyholders get older and die.

The end result of this formula is a premium which remains level throughout the lifetime of an individual. Even though his chances of death increase with age, the policyholder continues to pay the same amount each year.

The key to this system of calculations is the mortality table. Based on over one hundred years of study, actuaries can predict with uncanny accuracy the number of men within any age group who will live or die each succeeding year.

Using these studies of mortality of a group of men, all of the same age and all purchasing the same policy at the same time, the actuary is able to calculate the amount of money that must be available in any year to pay the death benefits for that year. He then determines how much more than the actual premium each man must pay in order to have enough reserves set aside for the higher risk in later years. These reserves, together with the premiums still being paid by survivors, will result in enough funds to pay death claims as they come due. Of every premium you pay, therefore, a portion of it is set aside to absorb your share of the higher losses and lower premium contributions in the later years.

Idle money is a wasting asset. With the exception of the estimated amount needed to pay claims that year, the sums set aside for reserves are not left idle. They are invested intelligently to swell the fund to a point where, again by mathematical calculation, their earnings can be used to reduce the share you would otherwise have been required to contribute.

One other factor enters the picture. The company has operating expenses such as agents' commissions, personnel salaries, home office operations, taxes, doctors' fees, and printing costs. A proportionate share of these expenses is added to the adjusted premium.

Your final premium, then, is composed of your over-all share of expected death claims, a proportionate share of the management expenses of the company, less your share of the earnings your funds bring in.

Obviously, this is an oversimplification of a most complicated concept. It should, however, indicate to you that sound investment practices, good mortality experience (less deaths per year than expected), and intelligent management have a direct influence on the premium you pay.

For the sake of safety, mortality figures are a bit overcalculated, investment earnings are conservatively figured, and operating expenses are usually overestimated.

In a stock company (one that does not return unused funds in the form of dividends to policyholders), savings derived from good mortality experience, from lower operating costs due to intelligent management, and excess earnings from sound investments are paid to stockholders as profits.

These same savings in a mutual company (one which has no stockholders) are returned proportionally to each policyholder as a refund commonly known as a dividend.

It is interesting to note that the share of the reserves that your premiums have helped to accumulate over the years in anticipation of your death becomes your guaranteed cash value which you can use for income at retirement age. You have lived long enough to remove yourself from the surviving group, and your reserves are no longer needed by the company to pay a death benefit. They can now be released to return either a lump sum or to pay you an income for as long as you live.

A recent development which influences the premium you must pay is the quantity discount. Whereas the share of company expenses was formerly figured at a particular sum for each $1,000 of insurance, it is now figured at a certain sum per policy. Thus, you would pay somewhat less for one $25,000 policy than you would for five $5,000 policies.

All companies must charge the same amount, based on a mortality table, for pure protection. Although investment practices also influence the ultimate premium you must pay, the day-by-day management and sales efficiency of the company usually account for variations in premiums. In the case of mutual companies, these variations are often reflected in the size of the dividends.

If a life insurance company discontinued all future operations, there would still be enough to pay all obligations to its present policyholders.

The insurance departments of all states keep an alert eye open for your protection. They see to it that the premium you pay is a fair one, considering all coverages, guarantees, and values involved.

TABLE 1 1958 CSO MORTALITY TABLE *

Commissioners Standard Ordinary

Age	Number Living	Number Dying	Death Rate Per 1,000	Expectancy, Years	Age	Number Living	Number Dying	Death Rate Per 1,000	Expectancy, Years
0	10,000,000	70,800	7.08	68.30	15	9,743,175	14,225	1.46	54.95
1	9,929,200	17,475	1.76	67.78	16	9,728,950	14,983	1.54	54.03
2	9,911,725	15,066	1.52	66.90	17	9,713,967	15,737	1.62	53.11
3	9,896,659	14,449	1.46	66.00	18	9,698,230	16,390	1.69	52.19
4	9,882,210	13,835	1.40	65.10	19	9,681,840	16,846	1.74	51.28
5	9,868,375	13,322	1.35	64.19	20	9,664,994	17,300	1.79	50.37
6	9,855,053	12,812	1.30	63.27	21	9,647,694	17,655	1.83	49.46
7	9,842,241	12,401	1.26	62.35	22	9,630,039	17,912	1.86	48.55
8	9,829,840	12,091	1.23	61.43	23	9,612,127	18,167	1.89	47.64
9	9,817,749	11,879	1.21	60.51	24	9,593,960	18,324	1.91	46.73
10	9,805,870	11,865	1.21	59.58	25	9,575,636	18,481	1.93	45.82
11	9,794,005	12,047	1.23	58.65	26	9,557,155	18,732	1.96	44.90
12	9,781,958	12,325	1.26	57.72	27	9,538,423	18,981	1.99	43.99
13	9,769,633	12,896	1.32	56.80	28	9,519,442	19,324	2.03	43.08
14	9,756,737	13,562	1.39	55.87	29	9,500,118	19,760	2.08	42.16

* Courtesy of Flitcraft Incorporated, New York, New York.

TABLE 1 1958 CSO MORTALITY TABLE—Continued

Age	Number Living	Number Dying	Death Rate Per 1,000	Expect-ancy, Years	Age	Number Living	Number Dying	Death Rate Per 1,000	Expect-ancy, Years
30	9,480,358	20,193	2.13	41.25	50	8,762,306	72,902	8.32	23.63
31	9,460,165	20,718	2.19	40.34	51	8,689,404	79,160	9.11	22.82
32	9,439,447	21,239	2.25	39.43	52	8,610,244	85,758	9.96	22.03
33	9,418,208	21,850	2.32	38.51	53	8,524,486	92,832	10.89	21.25
34	9,396,358	22,551	2.40	37.60	54	8,431,654	100,337	11.90	20.47
35	9,373,807	23,528	2.51	36.69	55	8,331,317	108,307	13.00	19.71
36	9,350,279	24,685	2.64	35.78	56	8,223,010	116,849	14.21	18.97
37	9,325,594	26,112	2.80	34.88	57	8,106,161	125,970	15.54	18.23
38	9,299,482	27,991	3.01	33.97	58	7,980,191	135,663	17.00	17.51
39	9,271,491	30,132	3.25	33.07	59	7,844,528	145,830	18.59	16.81
40	9,241,359	32,622	3.53	32.18	60	7,698,698	156,592	20.34	16.12
41	9,208,737	35,362	3.84	31.29	61	7,542,106	167,736	22.24	15.44
42	9,173,375	38,253	4.17	30.41	62	7,374,370	179,271	24.31	14.78
43	9,135,122	41,382	4.53	29.54	63	7,195,099	191,174	26.57	14.14
44	9,093,740	44,741	4.92	28.67	64	7,003,925	203,394	29.04	13.51
45	9,048,999	48,412	5.35	27.81	65	6,800,531	215,917	31.75	12.90
46	9,000,587	52,473	5.83	26.95	66	6,584,614	228,749	34.74	12.31
47	8,948,114	56,910	6.36	26.11	67	6,355,865	241,777	38.04	11.73
48	8,891,204	61,794	6.95	25.27	68	6,114,088	254,835	41.68	11.17
49	8,829,410	67,104	7.60	24.45	69	5,859,253	267,241	45.61	10.64

TABLE 1 1958 CSO MORTALITY TABLE—Continued

Age	Number Living	Number Dying	Death Rate Per 1,000	Expectancy, Years	Age	Number Living	Number Dying	Death Rate Per 1,000	Expectancy, Years
70	5,592,012	278,426	49.79	10.12	85	1,311,348	211,311	161.14	4.32
71	5,313,586	287,731	54.15	9.63	86	1,100,037	190,108	172.82	4.06
72	5,025,855	294,766	58.65	9.15	87	909,929	168,455	185.13	3.80
73	4,731,089	299,289	63.26	8.69	88	741,474	146,997	198.25	3.55
74	4,431,800	301,894	68.12	8.24	89	594,477	126,303	212.46	3.31
75	4,129,906	303,011	73.73	7.81	90	468,174	106,809	228.14	3.06
76	3,826,895	303,014	79.18	7.39	91	361,365	88,813	245.77	2.82
77	3,523,881	301,997	85.70	6.98	92	272,552	72,480	265.93	2.58
78	3,221,884	299,829	93.06	6.59	93	200,072	57,881	289.30	2.33
79	2,922,055	295,683	101.19	6.21	94	142,191	45,026	316.66	2.07
80	2,626,372	288,848	109.98	5.85	95	97,165	34,128	351.24	1.80
81	2,337,524	278,983	119.35	5.51	96	63,037	25,250	400.56	1.51
82	2,058,541	265,902	129.17	5.19	97	37,787	18,456	488.42	1.18
83	1,792,639	249,858	139.38	4.89	98	19,331	12,916	688.15	.83
84	1,542,781	231,433	150.01	4.60	99	6,415	6,415	1,000.00	.50

7. *Types of Policies*

The Tools of the Trade

Just as all cars in operating condition can get you to any destination, so do all life insurance policies have one thing in common: they provide a measure of family protection against your sudden death and before you have had the pleasure of raising your family and enjoying a lengthy retirement.

Just as there are many makes, sizes, and types of cars with variations to fit your particular needs and desires, so are there many types of policies with special provisions, called "riders," which are available to help you tailor-make a program to your particular needs.

Basically, all life insurance policies fall into one of three classifications:

1. Protection only
2. Protection with savings or investment features
3. Savings or investment with some protection

PROTECTION ONLY

Under this classification we find all term insurance policies. As the name implies, these policies cover you during a definite, predetermined number of years. These may be 1, 5, 10, 15, 20, 25, 30 years or to ages sixty-five or seventy. If death occurs during the chosen term of years, the company pays the amount for which you contracted. If you are alive at the end of those years, the policy expires and your protection ends. With very few exceptions, term policies do not have a cash value. Their use is strictly for death protection.

Many term policies provide either renewal or conversion privileges, or both. This means that at the expiration of a renewable and convertible five-year policy, for example, you may renew it for another five years, but you must pay the premiums due for your age at time of renewal. Usually, a policy may be renewed until age sixty-five, but each time at the premium rate based on your age at renewal. This renewal is automatic and does not require evidence of insurability.

The conversion privilege provides for a change of policy to a higher premium and equity-building type anytime before you become age sixty. This conversion is again effective without evidence of insurability. You usually pay the premium based on your age at the time of conversion. Some companies will permit you to pay all back premiums with interest and date your policy as of the original age of issue. There is hardly any reason for you to back-date and pay a large sum for coverage already received. You are better off in almost all instances to pay the premium as of the date of conversion. Even though it may be a higher one, due to your advanced age, you will be paying for fewer years and will not be tying up large sums of money which could be useful elsewhere.

Term insurance offers two variations: level and decreasing term. Level term keeps your protection at the original figure throughout the term period. If you own a level 20-year term policy, your beneficiaries will receive the full amount if death occurs anytime during the 20 years. Decreasing term provides for a sum that gradually decreases over a period of years.

Never before in the history of the insurance industry has so broad a selection of policies been made available to the buyer as there is today. Almost every need for temporary coverage can be satisfied.

The high cost of living has forced many professional men to supplement their protection programs with a variety of term policies and riders. Although these expire at some point in life and do not build equities, they do provide much-needed coverage for relatively low premiums. Many of the benefits described can be obtained as riders (provisions) attached to another policy at a premium reduction of up to 25 per cent of what their cost would be were they purchased as separate policies. This reduction is due to the fact that the company's expense of issuing a policy is absorbed by the basic plan and no additional expenses are incurred by the addition of the rider.

Here is a guide to most term policies available to you today:

Annual Renewable and Convertible Term

Each year you pay the premium called for at that age. You may renew the coverage each year for ten years with most companies without undergoing medical examinations.

Five- and Ten-Year Renewable and Convertible Term

Your premium remains the same for the five or ten years. At the end of those years, you may renew the policies for an additional five or ten years, but you must pay the premium based on your age at the time of renewal. These policies may be renewed until age sixty-five without medical examination. At that time, the coverage expires. You may convert the policy to any permanent type without evidence of insurability before age sixty-five.

Five-, Ten-, Fifteen-, Twenty-, Twenty-five-Year Convertible-Only Term

These are similar to those discussed except for the facts that they cannot be renewed and must be converted before the period of coverage is over.

Term to Sixty, Sixty-five, or Seventy

Unless earlier conversion is made, these policies expire at the preselected age. At any rate, no conversion can be made after age sixty-five.

Reducing Term from Ten to Forty Years

This coverage decreases at a predetermined rate until it eventually expires. For example, a $20,000 20-year decreasing term plan will have a death benefit of approximately $10,000 at the end of ten years. The plan expires at the end of the twentieth year.

FAMILY INCOME POLICY

This assures your family of a specific income until your children can become self-supporting. For example, a policy will provide for payment of $500 per month until the youngest child is eighteen years old, with payments commencing at the time of your death. Income ceases in the year in which the child reaches age eighteen. Actually, this is a form of reducing term insurance except that the benefits are in monthly payments instead of in a lump sum. For flexibility, all family income policies and riders make it possible for your family to collect a lump sum in lieu of income, but you must make written authorization to that effect during your lifetime. This is referred to as the "right of commutation." If this provision is not so indicated in either the original application or in a subsequent endorsement, your family must, after your death, accept preset monthly income payments, regardless of their needs.

JOINT TERM INSURANCE

Rarely written, and then only by very few companies, it covers two or more persons under one policy. The death benefit is paid when the first of the insured dies. This automatically terminates the coverage on all people concerned.

AUTOMATICALLY CONVERTIBLE TERM

This is similar to convertible-only policies, except that at the end of the term period it automatically converts to a whole life policy, thus leaving you no selection of plan. It does, however, prevent your permitting the coverage to expire due to lack of action on your part.

SINGLE PREMIUM DECREASING TERM

It provides the same benefits as regular decreasing term except that you pay the total required premium at one time. The over-all cost is greatly reduced because of the substantial discount you receive for making a single payment. However, you cannot cancel this type of policy if your need for it suddenly ends, nor are your payments returned if you die before the expiration of the term period.

Life Expectancy Term

Its coverage ends at your actuarially calculated life expectancy. For example, at age thirty-five it would grant you protection to age sixty-eight. This policy is rarely used since better coverage, such as term to seventy, can be obtained at approximately the same price.

Which form of term coverage should you buy?

This would be very easy to answer if you knew your date of death!

Term insurance should be used to fulfill a specific need.

Buy Short-Term (One to Five Years) Coverage If:

1. Your need for protection is great, but your funds are low.
2. You have short-term debts such as notes, equipment or student loans.
3. You have entered into a partnership and wish to fund a buy-out agreement at the least possible cost.*
4. You have aged parents depending on you, and you wish to provide for them for as long as they are alive.
5. You wish to guarantee your insurability (by conversion) for future purchases of permanent insurance.

Buy Long-Term (Ten Years or Longer) Coverage If:

1. You wish to save money in the over-all cost of term insurance. It is less expensive over a period of years because the premium you pay is an average over the span of years and does not increase when you get into the older ages.
2. You wish to increase your coverage during your peak earning and "need" years in order to combat creeping inflation which is constantly chipping away some dollar values of your regular life insurance program.

* See Chapter 30, "The Medical Partnership."

3. You wish to insure an educational fund for your children in case of your sudden death.

4. You wish to assure the availability of funds to complete an investment program in the event of your sudden death.

5. You wish to establish insurability for a purchase of permanent coverage in the future.

Buy Decreasing Term If:

1. You want the greatest amount of coverage immediately for the least amount of premium.

2. You have a decreasing obligation, such as a mortgage on your home or clinic.

3. You wish to provide monthly family income benefits expiring at a predetermined date at the lowest premium outlay.

4. You wish to establish insurability for a purchase of permanent coverage in the future.

Buy Joint Term If:

1. You and other physicians have a joint mortgage obligation on your clinic or professional building.

2. Both you and your wife wish to have your mortgage at home paid off when either dies.

When selecting any term plan, keep these points in mind:

1. Although the guarantee of renewability adds approximately 10 to 15 per cent to your premium for term coverage, it affords great flexibility in case your needs demand continuation of coverage beyond the original contract period.

2. Short-term is more expensive in the long run than, for example, coverage to age sixty-five. If, starting at age thirty-five, you renewed a five-year plan for thirty years, you would have paid a total of $4,578 at the end of that time. Had you purchased term to age sixty-five initially, your cost would have been $3,477. You would have effected a savings of $1,101, representing approximately 24 per cent. The initial purchase premium for short-term is lower, however, but increases each time you renew.

3. Add disability premium waiver to your term policy. Although very nominal in cost (approximately $4 a year on a $10,000 five-year renewable and convertible policy at age thirty-five), it obligates the insurance company to pay premiums for you during disability, until the policy comes up for renewal. Then, some companies will convert it to a whole life plan and will continue to pay the higher cost of the more valuable policy for you so long as you are disabled.

4. Many companies will issue term riders on term policies. This enables you to get a greater variety of coverage to meet specific needs at a very low cost. You can, for example, purchase $10,000 of ten-year renewable and convertible term (for education), and add a family income rider to provide $500 a month for the next ten years (for sustenance). In this way, you are not forced to purchase a more costly permanent policy in order to be permitted the addition of a family income rider.

5. Some companies even issue disability income riders with decreasing term. The nature of a disability income rider in life insurance, discussed in Chapter 17, will point out to you that this is not always a good buy.

6. If you apply for term insurance with the intention of converting at a later date, it is wise, at that time, to check into the permanent plans available with the same company, as you will eventually own one of them when you convert.

PERMANENT PROTECTION PLANS WITH SAVINGS FEATURES

The workhorse of life insurance is the whole life policy. Over 60 per cent of all policies bought consist of this form of coverage. The reason for its popularity is that it enables you to solve almost any insurance problem. It is also the least costly of all permanent insurance policies on the market.

As its name implies, the whole life policy is so designed actuarially that you pay a stipulated amount (level premium) for the rest of your life and receive coverage throughout your lifetime. Should you live to age one hundred, you would receive the insurance money yourself; otherwise, the death benefit is designed for your beneficiary.

How then, can you accomplish almost any purpose with whole life?

The secret lies in its remarkable flexibility. While you are paying premiums, you are also building up a cash reserve. Since your premium is relatively low, this reserve builds slowly. Yet, when you reach retirement age, enough value has accumulated to enable you to utilize this equity for income or other purposes. Let us study an illustration:

As a young man, age thirty-five, you are concerned with providing an income for your family in the event of your premature death. You are also thinking of your own old age and retirement. You can afford to set aside about $500 a year for these purposes.

You purchase $20,000 of whole life. This is enough to provide almost $200 a month income to your family for ten years from the date of your death. The odds, however, are in favor of your reaching retirement age sixty-five. At that age, you will have had 30 years of coverage. Your reserve values will have built up to approximately $11,000, and, if the policy were purchased from a participating (dividend-paying) company, accumulated dividends may amount to approximately $7,000. The total value of $18,000 not only exceeds your deposit of $15,000 by $3,000 but, more important, it can also give you an income of $1,271 per year for life with at least ten years guaranteed, or an income of $1,053 per year for life with at least 20 years guaranteed.

You had your cake (protection for the family), and you can eat it too (retirement for yourself).

Other permanent policies which we are about to investigate also accomplish both protection and retirement objectives, but always at the expense of one or the other. Only whole life gives the most protection when this protection is essential and yet returns enough toward retirement to make it the best buy of all policies for most family men.

Another popular plan is the 20 payment life. It is a duplicate of the whole life policy except that your premium is so calculated as to permit you to have the policy paid up with 20 annual premiums. Obviously, the premiums are higher than those for whole life. On the other hand, the reserves also build faster. You, the same thirty-five-year-old doctor, can use your $500 a year to purchase approximately $12,000 of twenty payment life. Your family gets less coverage ($8,000 less), or less income ($115 per month for ten years), and at retirement you receive $9,000 of cash value plus approximately $4,400 in dividends for a total of $13,400. This exceeds the total 20 premium deposits of $10,000 by $3,400, but will only bring an income after age sixty-five of $947 a year for life with ten years guaranteed or $784 a year for life with 20 years guaranteed. On the other hand, you made only 20 deposits, in this case until age fifty-five, and paid no premiums at all to age sixty-five. On a profit comparison, you would come out better with a twenty payment life policy, even though you paid in ten years less premium than on whole life. But, because this slight advantage would cost you $8,000 of coverage you did not receive, you should prefer the whole life to a 20 payment life policy. The same holds true with other forms of life policies for which premium payments are limited to 10, 25, or 30 years or to ages sixty, sixty-five, or seventy. Only the ratio of coverage purchased by your premium changes. The fewer your years of premium payment, the less your coverage purchased. Here is a breakdown:

WHAT $500 A YEAR WILL PURCHASE AT AGE 35:

Type of Policy	*Approximate Death Benefit*
Whole Life	$20,000
Life Paid Up at Sixty-Five	17,500
Endowment at Sixty-Five	15,200
Twenty Payment Life	12,000
Retirement Income at Sixty-Five	10,700
Twenty Year Endowment	10,000
Ten Payment Life	8,000
Retirement Income at Sixty	7,600
Retirement Income at Fifty-Five	5,300
Ten Year Endowment	4,700

Most insurance companies also issue "specials" which are designed either to serve an unusual purpose or to make the product more marketable.

Joint life insurance is a single policy issued on the lives of two people, usually husband and wife or business partners. The insurance money is paid to the survivor when the first death occurs. This payment terminates the policy. The premium is based on the average age of the two insureds, and special tables of mortality and benefits are used. The premium is about 70 per cent of what it would have cost had each insured taken out a separate policy on his life. If both policyholders live to old age, the joint life plan provides for joint cash and joint retirement values, exactly as any other policy. However, all actions regarding the benefits must be agreed upon by both insureds. In order for one to cash in the policy, the other must agree. In order for one to receive life income, the other must agree and also accept life income. A beneficiary arrangement cannot be made or altered without joint consent. A loan must be executed by both.

This lack of flexibility, added to the fact that the survivor loses all insurance protection, makes the joint life plan a relatively unpopular one. It is most useful in the case of a husband and wife who have no heirs and where the only concern is the continued financial well-being of the surviving mate. Joint life can serve that purpose efficiently and economically. Professional partnerships should avoid this plan because of its inflexibility. A disagreement or breakup of the partnership can create many unnecessary insurance problems. Furthermore, most surviving physicians would want to retain rather than lose their share of partnership insurance since, with a proper change of beneficiary, it could enhance their personal programs.

Another special policy is the modified life plan, a policy for the young man of small means. You pay a low premium for either one, two, three, or five years, and then an increased amount for the life of the policy. If you do not wish to pay the increase, you will have your insurance reduced accordingly.

The advantage of the modified life plan lies in the fact that it begins to build some equity in the initial stages and offers you a policy you are less likely to drop than term insurance. It is a package that requires little action on your part. The increase in premium (which, in effect, is a conversion from one type of insurance to another) is automatic. There are no papers to sign, no decisions to make.

Remember, however, that if you are looking for low premiums in the initial stages of your program, pure one-, two-, three-, or five-year term will do the job more economically.

Another insurance package is the double protection plan for 20 years or to age sixty-five. This can provide coverage for $10,000 during the next 20 years or, if the company issues it, to age sixty-five. Thereafter, the coverage is reduced to $5,000. A good salesman will emphasize that it is a $5,000 policy that affords double the protection for a stipulated number of years. Stripped of all oratory, this plan is $5,000 of whole life with 20-year term or term to sixty-five added to it. Since only the basic permanent policy builds equity, you may be better off purchasing term separately, either as a policy or rider. Many companies specialize in term insurance and will give you the double protection at a substantial savings over the above-mentioned package plan.

A relatively new and useful concept is the graded premium or increasing premium plan. This is a whole life policy which provides for a lower initial premium, with a gradual annual increase over five or ten years. A thirty-year-old physician interested in a ten-year graded premium contract would purchase a $25,000 policy for an initial premium of $341.50 a year. This would increase about $25 annually until, at age forty-one, his premium would level out at $589 a year. This would equal the regular premium he would have had to pay starting with age thirty-four. However, he is able to begin on a substantial permanent and equity-building program early. As his practice grows, he is able to absorb gradual premium increases much more easily than sudden jumps.

Before you purchase any special policy, try to determine if it is one devised to serve a specific purpose or if it is just a merchandising package, the results of which you can equal or better with other policies or companies. Be especially concerned with the flexibility of special policies. Sometimes, a penny saved is just trouble earned.

Buy Whole Life Insurance If:

1. You want the largest amount of permanent coverage for your premium dollar.

2. You want the most flexible coverage. It is simple to change a whole life policy to a higher premium type, but it may be impossible to change from retirement income to whole life, since evidence of insurability is required at the time of the change.

3. You want your premium dollar to work for both your protection and savings.

4. You want permanent coverage, yet wish to release premiums you would normally put into higher cost policies for other speculative types of investments or for spendable income.

5. You want to create ready cash funds for estate taxes and other cleanup purposes.

Buy Limited Payment (Such as Twenty Payment) Life If:

1. Your need for protection is not too great. This refers especially to the single man.

2. Your retirement plans call for most of your obligations to be paid up at a certain age. If you plan to retire at age fifty-five, for instance, you may want your policies paid up for their full value at that age.

3. Your peak earning years are limited and you want to pay off your policy before your income declines.

PERMANENT SAVINGS PLANS WITH PROTECTION FEATURES

Endowment and retirement policies are especially designed to provide either a lump sum or monthly income at a certain date. A twenty year endowment for $10,000 will give you, at age thirty-five, 20 years of coverage in the amount of $10,000 and will return to you, at age fifty-five, $10,000 of cash plus accumulated dividends. Since your premium would be about $510 per year, this is certainly no bargain as an investment or as protection. It is, however, a forced savings program and does guarantee a definite sum at a definite time.

Retirement income policies are similar to endowments, but are constructed so as to accumulate enough savings to enable the insurance company to guarantee a fixed income for life.*

Again, this is a forced savings program, but it has the additional advantage of guaranteeing an income which you cannot outlive.

Endowments can be bought for 5, 10, 18, 20, 25, or 30 years or

* See Chapter 26, "Policies Designed for Retirement."

to ages sixty and sixty-five. Retirement income policies are available to begin paying income at ages fifty-five, sixty, sixty-five, or seventy.

Endowment and retirement income policies are the most expensive you can buy. They also represent the least risk to the insurance company. Unless your basic protection program is nearly complete, or you have a specific reason, you have no business owning an endowment or retirement income policy.

Buy Endowment And/Or Retirement Income Policies If:

1. You cannot save money regularly.
2. You do not have the time, patience, know-how, or temperament to invest elsewhere.
3. You want to be assured that a definite sum will be available for a definite purpose at a definite time. If you save $500 a year in a bank for your son's education regularly, you may as well put it into an endowment policy and receive coverage too.
4. You want a basic fixed retirement income which you cannot outlive. This may be the only income you will receive or it may be that foundation toward retirement which will be supplemented by income from other investment sources.
5. Your personal protection program is complete and coverage is no longer important.

When purchasing any permanent policies, remember these points:

1. Your family's security comes first.
2. The more permanent insurance you purchase toward your family's security, the more equity you will build toward your own retirement.
3. The larger the premium you pay for each $1,000 of protection, the less protection you receive. For example, a $10,000 policy costing you $500 a year reduces the actual death benefits assumed by the insurance company by that much per year. After ten years, you have invested $5,000. If you die at that point, your widow gets that $5,000 plus another $5,000 from the company. Although this factor is considered in calculating premiums and cash values, it is still wise to obtain as much company risk as possible by purchasing whole life insurance.
4. All permanent policies have paid-up values. If, at age thirty-five,

you purchase $20,000 of whole life coverage for approximately $500 a year, this policy may, at the end of 20 years, be exchanged for one that is paid up for approximately $10,000. Throughout the 20-year period, however, you have enjoyed the protection of $20,000. Had you bought a twenty payment life plan, you would also have paid $500 per year but for $12,000 of coverage, and you would have a $12,000 policy paid up at the end of 20 years.

Using whole life, you have benefited by two-thirds more coverage for 20 years, but have lost one-sixth under paid-up insurance. Your needs usually are greater while you are young and raising a family. Thus, even though you end up with only $10,000 of paid-up insurance, the additional coverage you enjoyed during the years you needed it most is certainly a compensating factor.

5. Most economists will agree that your retirement program should consist of a combination of fixed income through insurance, and variable income from other investments. By assuring your family of adequate coverage through the use of permanent insurance, you will automatically establish that portion of your retirement plan which should be in the form of fixed income. Conversely, any fixed retirement income you establish through insurance will automatically enhance the security program of your family.

6. Your agent will undoubtedly bring up the factor of net cost. Generally, this is intended to show that after you deduct dividends from premiums and compare the total paid in to the cash value available, your actual cost, by the time you are ready to retire, will have been either very small or none at all, or you will have made a profit. If you live to retire and use the policy as income, this net-cost picture is meaningful. Remember, however, that if you die, your widow receives the face value of your policy regardless of how much or how little you have paid in. Furthermore, if you leave your policy as a paid-up one with the company, for various tax and other future needs, comparisons and calculations of cash values once again mean nothing, since only the face amount will be paid upon your death. Net cost is usually based largely on dividend estimates. Since dividends are never guaranteed, the final figures may be quite different from those shown you when you first bought the policy. Therefore, purchase the policy that has the most favorable aspects based on your actual needs, and don't let a percentage point, one way or the

other, in net-cost calculations sway you from that policy, company, and agent who can help you solve your problems now.

7. Investigate the advisability of adding term riders to your permanent plan. While you are purchasing a permanent insurance policy, it may pay you to consolidate several term policies you may now be carrying into one or two term riders.

8. Once you own a permanent policy, it is usually not advantageous to lapse it in order to purchase another policy. Most of the expenses, such as commissions, doctors' fees, taxes, issue fees, have already been paid from your first year's premium. By dropping one to take another, you will again pay a first-year premium which will be used to cover the same expenses. This will influence your immediate and future cash values and other benefits. In some instances a change is necessary, but this is indeed rare.

8. *Standard Provisions*

What You Will Find in Your Policy

The insurance agent had come at a most inopportune time to deliver the policy. Dr. Benson's waiting room was unexpectedly crowded. But the doctor always honored an appointment. He had the agent sent in.

"Nice to see you again," Dr. Benson began, "but, as you can see, I am a bit crowded for time. Suppose you just leave the policy for me to look over. If I have any questions, I can call you."

The agent smiled. "Sorry, I can't go along with you, Dr. Benson. This policy contains a lot more than a promise to feed your family. I want to be certain that you are aware of all privileges, benefits, and, incidentally, restrictions. Suppose I come by again next week?"

Dr. Benson shook his hand. "Please have lunch with me on Monday and we'll go over the policy then."

There are certain standard clauses most insurance buyers skip over when they receive their new policies. Many of these conditions and benefits are of little importance to your over-all financial picture, yet some can be significant. It will be well worth your while to acquaint yourself with these standard provisions and their meanings.

On the first page of the policy, called "face," you will find the name of the company, the policy number, your age when the policy was issued, your name, the sum of insurance provided, the names of your beneficiaries, the premium and how it is payable, and the date the insurance became effective. Below that, you will find a synopsis of the basic contents of your policy.

The synopsis will indicate the technical name of the policy, the length of time the premiums must be paid, when death benefits are payable, if dividends can be expected, and what other additional benefits may be included in the policy. This short description can serve as an instant spot check on the contents of your policy.

Within the policy itself, you will find the following standard provisions, not necessarily in the order as shown here, but essentially with the same meaning. There will be provisions covering:

Policy Ownership

This indicates the rights and privileges accorded the owner of the policy including the right to cash it in, change the beneficiary, and borrow against it.

Assignments

You have the right to assign the values and ownership of your policy to someone else either permanently or temporarily. However, you must send the company a copy of such legal assignment.

Beneficiary

In this clause you will find all the conditions relating to your right, or lack of right, to change the beneficiary of your policy. It also outlines the liability of the company in the event the designated beneficiary is no longer alive and no new beneficiary has been named.

Premiums

This clause shows how premiums are payable and to whom they are payable. It also indicates whether or not the company will return any unused premium after your death, or if it will charge the balance of the premium for that year. If neither of these is mentioned, it usually means that the company will neither return nor charge any further premiums at time of death.

Grace Period

A 31-day grace period for the payment of every premium is guaranteed in this provision. It further states that the unpaid premium due will be deducted from the benefits in the event that death occurs during the grace period.

LAPSE AND REINSTATEMENT

This provision defines the action that must be taken if you wish to reinstate a policy which has lapsed because of nonpayment of premium. It further shows under what conditions the company will accept the application for reinstatement.

DIVIDENDS

In a participating contract, this clause refers to the uses that you may make of any dividends which may be credited to you. This includes a dividend payment in cash, as a reduction of premiums, purchase of additional paid-up insurance, an accumulation at interest, and, in some instances, a purchase of additional yearly term insurance.* An interest factor is mentioned in that part of the clause dealing with dividend accumulations. It pertains to the minimum amount of interest your accumulations will earn. At the present time, companies are paying well in excess of this minimum guarantee.

THE CONTRACT

This provision states that the policy and all papers attached to it constitute the entire contract between the parties.

SUICIDE

The company does not assume any liability if you commit suicide within two years from the date of issue. If you do, it is obligated only to return the premiums actually paid. After two years, suicide is covered.

INCONTESTABILITY

This assures you that once the policy is two years old, the company cannot contest it for any reason whatever. Some policies ex-

* See Chapter 23, "Dividends—Use Dividends to Best Advantage."

clude from this incontestability clause any benefits pertaining to disability and accidental death.

Age

If your age was misstated at the time of purchase, the benefits will be adjusted to those which your premium would have purchased at your correct age.

Policy Loans

This clause discusses the conditions under which you may obtain a loan, how much you may receive, when you may receive it, the amount of interest you must pay, and the method of repayment.

Nonforfeiture Options—Options on Surrender or Lapse of Policy

This provision contains three parts. The first part indicates that in the event you must discontinue your policy, you may take the policy's cash value, reduced paid-up insurance, or additional term insurance for a given number of years.* It further provides that one of these three methods, usually the additional term insurance, will go into effect automatically if you have not indicated any choice. Another section describes the legal basis by which these cash, paid-up, and term insurance values are computed. The third section is a chart in which the figures are given for each of the three surrender values in any given year.

Settlement Options

This clause, usually from one to two pages long, describes in detail the many ways in which you or your beneficiary can receive the proceeds of the policy. It has charts to give exact guaranteed figures for each one of these methods of settlement. This clause is by far the most important in your contract. It will show, for example,

*See Chapter 15, "Nonforfeiture Values—What Happens When You Stop Paying on Your Life Insurance?"

the amount of interest your company will pay if you or your beneficiary decide to leave proceeds on deposit for a later "pay off." The tables will further show the amount of monthly income that is guaranteed if the proceeds are divided equally over a certain number of years. Additional tables indicate the amount of life income, with or without guaranteed periods, that are available to you or your beneficiaries at any given age. Because of the importance of this provision, a detailed explanation can be found in Chapter 12, "Settlement Options—The Pay Off."

PREMIUM LOAN

This provision safeguards your policy against unintentional lapse. It specifies that in the event a premium is not paid, the company will automatically lend that amount of premium and will consider it exactly as if you had gone through formal loan procedures. The premium loan can be repaid exactly as any normal loan.

AUTHORITY

No one, other than an officer of a company, has the authority to agree to modify or change the contract in any way whatever.

ENDORSEMENTS

Usually there is a blank space in the policy for changes or endorsements that may be made relating to beneficiary designations, settlement options, method of premium payment, and additions and subtractions to the policy.

Special attention should be paid to those provisions relating to interest paid by the company on accumulated dividends, interest charged on loans from the company, and the values afforded under settlement options. These are the provisions that you are most likely to encounter at some time during your life.

From time to time, state statutes require that certain benefits or clauses be included in all life insurance policies for the protection of the policyholder. Companies abide by state statutes and incorporate such changes automatically into their existing as well as new policies.

9. *The Quality Policy*

It's the Difference That Counts

All life insurance contracts contain standard clauses. They begin to differ, however, in certain other aspects that can serve as quick, spot-checking devices to determine the over-all quality of a policy. These are the points of difference among the major companies who sell most of the insurance in the United States. Depending upon particular desires and needs, one of these four points may enhance your insurance program considerably.

Let us discuss each point in detail and study the impact it may have on your future.

1. Since all permanent insurance policies can be used for retirement, and since all policies, whether permanent or not, can be used for income to a beneficiary, two most important provisions in your policy are the annuity factor and the monthly income charts.* They both show the guaranteed amount of income the company will pay as death or retirement benefits. Some companies differ sharply in the amount of income they will return to their policyholders, sometimes by as much as 10 per cent.

The higher the annuity factor in your policy, the more income you will receive at retirement time. The higher the income factor in your policy, the more your beneficiary will receive if you die before retirement.

These factors and charts are easy to find in any existing or proposed policy under the heading "Optional Modes of Settlement."

2. There may come a time when you find it necessary to borrow

* See Chapters 12 and 25, "Settlement Options—The Pay Off" and "The Pension Power of Your Life Insurance," respectively.

money from the insurance company, using your policy as collateral. In your contract, listed under the heading "Loan Values," the company indicates the guaranteed interest rate you will be charged when you borrow. Most companies will charge anywhere from 4 to 6 per cent. Knowing of this benefit, you will be able to determine from which company it is most profitable for you to borrow. If you have recent policies, you may find it more advisable to use them as collateral, rather than old policies.*

3. As the years roll on, your original insurance objectives may change. For example, you needed low-cost and low-equity types of coverage while you were raising a family. Later, with the children on their own, you may want to concentrate on preparations for your retirement. If your policy contains a change of plan clause, you will be guaranteed the right to increase the pension power of your insurance by converting the policy to one that places greater emphasis on cash accumulation. Conversely, you may have purchased high-cost and high-equity policies only to find, in later years, that you need more protection than these policies extend. You may then convert to a lower-cost plan. This reduces your premium. The difference in premiums thus released can pay for the additional coverage you need to purchase.†

Even if your policy does not contain the change of plan clause, the company may permit these adjustments if you are still insurable. However, the inclusion of such a clause puts you in control and affords you the opportunity to plan necessary changes under contractual and clearly stated, rather than unknown and changeable conditions.

4. Most physicians pay their insurance on an annual basis. Many of them are not aware of the fact that in the event they die at the beginning of the year, some insurance companies will keep the balance of the premium, even though it has been literally unearned. Some companies actually charge for the full year regardless of your usual mode of payment. Thus, if you pay a quarterly premium and die during that quarter, those particular companies will deduct the balance of the yearly premium before they will pay the death benefit

* See Chapter 24, "Loan Values—When to Borrow On Your Life Insurance."

† See Chapter 22, "The Change of Plan Clause—You Can Change Your Policy."

to your beneficiary. Many companies return the amount of premium that has not been used. Needless to say, of greatest advantage to you is that policy which provides a return of the unused portion of your premium in the event of death. The most important reason for paying a premium annually is the savings involved. Coupled with this return of premium guarantee, it is the safest method of paying annual premiums. If the company does not return any premiums paid in advance, the savings effected by annual payment may be wiped out. If a company deducts the balance of the annual premium, your death benefit will be reduced by the balance of that annual premium regardless of how you pay it.

These four check points, annuity and income factors, loan interest, change of plan provisions, and premium adjustment, can quickly give you an indication as to the over-all quality of the policy and the intent of the company. Obviously, there are many other important features that will influence your particular program. Those listed, however, should serve as simple guides.

10. *Insurance Needs*

How Much and What Kind Do You Really Need?

"How much coverage do I really need?" is one of the first questions that enters the insurance buyer's mind.

There is no formula or guide that applies to everyone. The amount and type of coverage you own will be greatly influenced by your philosophy of life, your affection for your family, your desire for security, your income, your state of health, the state of health of your family, your background, and your ambitions. You must remember that insurance is not the only way you can provide for your family's security. If, for instance, you receive a regular income from an inheritance, this income is, in a way, a form of family maintenance insurance. The more income-producing and liquid assets you own, the less your need for insurance.

Here, then, is one way of determining the actual amount of coverage you should own.

Here are the basic needs of *all* men:

1. Last Expenses

Funeral, debts, taxes, installments due, medical expenses, student loans.

2. Readjustment Income

Enough to provide replacement of normal income to give the family time to adjust to a lower standard of living, if necessary.

3. Mortgage Cancellation

A sum to pay off the mortgage, buy another home, or serve as rent payments.

4. Dependency Income

Money to provide income while the children are in their minority.

5. Wife Income

An amount payable to your wife for as long as she lives, to give her a measure of security and independence.

6. Education

Funds to enable your wife to put the children through college and/or professional schools.

7. Emergency

A lump sum upon which your family can draw in an emergency or if an unusual opportunity arises.

8. Retirement

A life income for you and your wife.

On a sheet of paper, list these basic needs in the order of their importance to *you*. Next to each item, enter the minimum amount that you feel is required to satisfy those needs. The total of the eight items equals the liquid assets necessary to accomplish your desires.

Let us look at the list of one doctor whose age is thirty-five, whose wife's age is the same, and who has two sons, ages six and five.

1. Last expenses	$ 5,000
2. Emergency	10,000
3. Readjustment ($800 mo. for 1 year)	9,600
4. Mortgage ($25,000—20-yr. mortgage)	25,000
5. Dependency income ($500 mo. for 15 yrs.)	90,000
6. Wife income ($200 mo. for life starting at 62)	50,000
7. Education (2 boys, $8,000 each)	16,000
Total assets required for security	$205,600
8. Retirement ($500 mo. starting at 65.) Total cash needed to produce $500 a month through the cash value and dividend accumulations of the policies purchased for family protection	$ 90,000

This list indicates that this particular physician should own about $90,000 of permanent insurance. This will guarantee the last expenses, emergency, wife income, cash equity for education, and retirement funds, all of which are permanent needs, requiring cash values and having an unpredictable date of commencement or termination. The other needs, i.e., readjustment, mortgage, and dependency income, being of a temporary nature, can be satisfied by term insurance. If you own other assets, you may be able to reduce your over-all need for coverage. Good securities, safe mortgages, income from trusts, saleable office equipment, or a partnership equity may produce enough income to provide all or part of the listed needs. Your coverage can, therefore, be reduced accordingly. Keep in mind, however, that the financial independence of your family leaves no room for speculation. The needs outlined were basic minimum ones. Most experts agree that it is wise to establish through insurance a full program based on minimum needs, and to utilize other assets to enhance these minimums. You would then be certain that your policies would provide the absolute necessities, while your other assets would add a few luxuries and/or compensate for the inflationary tendency in our economy.

Few physicians at age thirty-five have had enough time to build assets large enough and strong enough to take the place of an insurance estate, which can be created with the stroke of a pen.

If you cannot afford to pay for a complete program, cover those needs you listed first in any way possible even if it means buying a large amount of term and very little of permanent coverage. A widow with children needs money. Any protection that you intend to purchase later does not put meat and potatoes on the table if you don't live long enough to carry out your intention.

DETERMINE YOUR OWN INSURANCE NEEDS

1. Last Expense Fund .... $______
   (Adjust amount downward if you have major medical coverage, cash in the bank, easily redeemable bonds.)
2. Emergency Fund .... $______
   (Deduct unallocated cash, government bonds, and the like.)
3. Readjustment Fund: $____ a year for ____ yrs. ...... $______
   (Deduct steady income derived from trust funds, property, rentals, mortgages, investments.)
4. Mortgage Fund .... $______
   (Keep in mind value of equity and the possibility that the family may want to move to smaller or less expensive quarters.)

5. Dependency Income: $____yr. for ____ yrs. ....$______
   (Provide enough to see children through college, deduct steady income derived from sources mentioned in #3.)
6. Wife Income: $____yr., starting with wife's age ____* .$______
7. Education † ....$______
   (Consider costs of schools most likely to be attended and probable rise of tuition fees. Needs are less if dependency income is made available and local schools are attended.)
8. Retirement,‡ $____yr., starting with agc ____ ....$______
   (Deduct income from other sources. Remember that the permanent portion of your protection program will automatically enhance your retirement picture. Thus, include any permanent insurance cash values in policies used for #1, 2, 6, and 7 in your calculations.)
   Total Coverage Needed: ....$______

* For each $10,000 of death benefit, your wife can receive the following life income (ten years guaranteed) starting with the listed ages: (Varies slightly with different companies.)

Wife's Age	*Yearly Income*	*Monthly Income*
50	$460.30	$39.10
55	507.00	43.20
60	564.60	48.20
62	591.30	50.50
65	636.30	54.40

† Education coverage consisting of term insurance will only provide sufficient money if you die. Using permanent insurance, you will protect your children if you die, but, in addition, you will build equity which you can use for tuition. If you can put the children through school out of earned income, you can continue to own the policies intended for education and let their equities enhance your later retirement income.

‡ For every $10,000 of equity (cash values and accumulated dividends), you can receive the following life income (ten years guaranteed), at the listed ages. (Varies slightly with different companies.)

Retirement Age	*Yearly Income*	*Monthly Income*
50	$496.90	$42.30
55	552.00	47.10
60	620.70	53.00
62	652.70	55.80
65	706.20	60.40

Amount of permanent insurance required:
Total of #1, 2, 6, and 7 ....$______
Amount of permanent insurance now in force .$______
Additional Permanent Insurance Needed: ....$______
Amount of term insurance required:
Total of #3, 4, and 5 ....$______
Amount of term now in force ....$______
Additional Term Insurance Needed: ....$______

11. *Paying Premiums*

Is the Convenience Worth the Penalty?

Dr. Benson had a choice. He could pay the premium yearly, twice a year, every three months, or monthly.

He calculated:

		Penalty
Annual Premium	$371.30	
Semiannual = $191.20 twice	382.40	3%
Quarterly = $97.50 four times	390.00	5%
Monthly = $32.80 twelve times	393.60	6%

It didn't take long to decide. He made out a check for $371.30.

Always pay your premiums annually if you can. You save approximately 6 per cent over the monthly method because the company has less administrative expenses and bookkeeping entries, and has longer use of more of your money.

Some advisors have suggested that, instead of purchasing one $40,000 policy and paying it quarterly (at a penalty of approximately 5 per cent), you should purchase four $10,000 policies, one every three months, and pay these annually. This advice, however, contains three dangerous fallacies.

1. You may die before completing the purchase of all four policies.
2. You may become uninsurable and find yourself unable to complete the purchase.
3. You will most certainly pay some premiums at the next higher age.

Here are some points to keep in mind:

1. You can overcome the aforementioned problem by purchasing four $10,000 policies payable on a quarterly basis. At the end of the first quarter pay one of the policies annually, at the end of the second quarter pay another annually, and do the same at the end of the other two quarters. This assures you of the coverage immediately, but conveniently spaces your premiums, eventually allowing you to pay on an annual basis at less cost than paying quarterly on all four policies.

2. Sometimes the desirability of budgeting your premium payments conveniently is worth the extra cost.

3. Withdraw the full annual premium from your savings account. Establish another savings account, designating it for insurance premiums only. Then, each month or quarter, deposit into that account the exact premium you would have had to send to the insurance company. At the next premium due date, withdraw the annual premium and start your deposits over again. You gain both by the savings effected on the annual premium method and by the interest your self-imposed monthly "premiums" earn in your savings account. After many years, you will find enough savings accumulated in the account to equal a full annual premium. Obviously, this method is only possible if you have a savings account, can spare the initial amount involved, and have the strength of character to deposit what would have been monthly or quarterly premiums.

4. Your company may employ an automatic check or bank draft plan. This affords you the convenience of monthly premium payments with the savings you would normally have received had you paid semiannually.

With this method, you authorize the company to issue a monthly draft against your checking account in the amount of the premium. Your bank statement serves as a reminder to deduct this amount from your balance. The company receives its money promptly and without the expense of premium notices. You, on the other hand, are relieved of writing checks, facing the danger of a policy lapse due to an oversight, and you benefit by the convenience of monthly budgeting with advantageous "semiannual" savings.

Your bank must be willing to cooperate. If it is not, it may be worthwhile to open an account for this purpose in another bank.

Often, the savings effected by this method exceed any bank charges made to maintain the account.

5. The postdated check plan can sometimes be used to advantage. You pay your premium with 12 postdated checks. The monthly premium is calculated to give you the savings of a semiannual premium. Each month the company deposits one check. You must, however, be sure to notify the company at once if you ever intend to change banks.

6. You can pay premiums for years in advance. You receive a 3 to 4 per cent discount. Should you suddenly die, the company will return to your beneficiary the unused portion of your money. Should you need the money paid for advance premiums, you can get it back with interest. If you are in a high income tax bracket, your greatest advantage in paying premiums well in advance lies in the fact that the discount earned in this way is not considered current taxable income.

Thus, it represents an investment earning of 3 or 4 per cent after taxes. In order to realize similar earnings after taxes, you must gross the following:

Top Federal Income Tax Bracket Per Cent	*Yield Before Taxes Necessary to Net 3 Per Cent After Taxes Per Cent*
20	3.75
30	4.29
50	6.00
70	10.00
	To Net 4 Per Cent After Taxes
20	5.00
30	5.71
50	8.00
70	13.33

7. You may pay all premiums at one time and save a substantial sum. At age thirty-five, you would receive $10,000 of paid-up coverage for life for a single premium of about $5,300. Using a twenty payment life policy, it would require 20 annual payments of $390, or

a total of $7,800 to have the same $10,000 of paid-up coverage. Again, this discount is not considered current taxable income.

One drawback to the single premium plan lies in the fact that there is no return made of unused premiums if you die in the early years. Thus, your beneficiary receives the $10,000 for which you paid $5,300. Had you purchased a twenty payment life, the same death benefit would be paid even though you may have only made one premium deposit of $390.

8. A few companies offer the premium deposit fund. It permits you to deposit small amounts, whenever you so desire, for future annual premium payments. Suppose your annual premium is $600. You can send the company $50 a month or any irregular amount which will accumulate to at least $600 over the period of a year. When your next annual premium is due, the company will take it from the deposit fund. This method has enabled you to pay your premiums monthly or even irregularly while still enjoying the discount of an annual premium. Monies in the deposit fund draw anywhere from 2 to 4 per cent in interest.

RELATIONSHIP OF PREMIUMS TO COVERAGE

Dr. Benson, age 35, had two close friends in the life insurance business. He called both to his home one evening and said:

"I need more permanent coverage for protection and retirement. Here, Joe, is a check for $500; and here, Bill, is a check for $500. Get me whatever policy is best for me."

The agents filled out the papers and examinations were arranged. The policies were issued and delivered to Dr. Benson. He didn't even bother to look them over, since his confidence in both men was strong.

A year later, Dr. Harry Benson was killed in an automobile accident. Both agents commiserated with the widow. Agent Joe informed her that she was entitled to $10,000 in lump sum or $95 a month for ten years from his company. Agent Bill informed her that she was entitled to $20,000 in lump sum or $190 a month for ten years from his company.

The widow clearly remembered that her husband had given each *man $500 for insurance. She demanded to know why Agent Joe's policy only provided for one half of what Agent Bill's called for.*

"Well," explained Joe, "had he lived to age sixty-five, he would have received more retirement income from my policy."

The wise insurance buyer purchases as much permanent risk as possible for his premium dollar. The flexibility in most policies makes it possible for him to make adjustments as he goes along.

The following chart presents a comparison analysis of various policies at the same premium and their values at certain points in life:

TABLE 2 WHAT A PREMIUM OF $420 A YEAR WILL PURCHASE

			Cash Value and Estimated Dividends:		
Age	*Policy*	*Amount of Insurance*	*10 yr.*	*20 yr.*	*Age 65*
30	Whole Life	$20,570	$3,766	$ 9,697	$21,265
	20 Pay Life	13,000	4,150	10,490	16,210
	Ret. Inc. @ 65	11,100	4,125	10,460	25,000
35	Whole Life	17,650	3,765	9,450	16,280
	20 Pay Life	11,500	4,038	9,460	14,630
	Ret. Inc. @ 65	8,850	4,100	10,400	19,190
40	Whole Life	14,950	3,690	9,050	12,070
	20 Pay Life	10,250	3,942	9,850	11,321
	Ret. Inc. @ 65	6,990	4,150	10,480	14,555
45	Whole Life	12,450	3,560	8,573	8,573
	20 Pay Life	9,000	3,790	9,395	9,395
	Ret. Inc. @ 65	5,300	4,220	10,585	10,585

12. *Settlement Options*

The Pay Off

Many policy owners and prospective insurance buyers seem to neglect, or are unaware of, the single most important benefit their policy provides. Because of this lack of awareness, policyholders have lost or voluntarily given up millions of dollars which their families could have received. Furthermore, additional millions have been misdirected and countless plans and ambitions have been destroyed because settlement options were not utilized to their greatest advantage.

Every permanent policy provides within the contract that a beneficiary, or recipient of insurance dollars, may receive these in other than lump sum.

Here are some of the different ways by which benefits may be collected:

On Interest Only

Monies may be left with the company for a specific period of time or indefinitely. While these benefits are with the company, your beneficiary may receive monthly, quarterly, semiannual or annual interest payments. Any sums not collected by the beneficiary would, upon her death, be payable to a second beneficiary or heir.

Limited Installments

Insurance dollars may be withdrawn over a stipulated period of time, ranging anywhere from 1 to 30 years. The income paid is larger than the mathematical division of the amount of money into the number of years because that balance of the money still to be collected earns interest.

TABLE 3 MONTHLY PAYMENTS FOR EACH $1000 OF PROCEEDS APPLIED

INCOME FOR A FIXED PERIOD					
Period of Years	*Payment*	*Period of Years*	*Payment*	*Period of Years*	*Payment*
1	$84.28	11	$8.64	21	$5.08
2	42.66	12	8.02	22	4.90
3	28.79	13	7.49	23	4.74
4	21.86	14	7.03	24	4.60
5	17.70	15	6.64	25	4.46
6	14.93	16	6.30	26	4.34
7	12.95	17	6.00	27	4.22
8	11.47	18	5.73	28	4.12
9	10.32	19	5.49	29	4.02
10	9.39	20	5.27	30	3.93

Annual, semiannual or quarterly payments under this option are 11.865, 5.969 and 2.994 respectively times the monthly payments.

Fixed Installments

Your policy may be so set up as to provide definite amounts of monthly income until all monies have been exhausted. Once again, the balance that has not been withdrawn earns interest and that interest extends the length of time the benefits can be received.

Life Income

Income may be received by the beneficiary for life with 5, 10, 15, or 20 years guaranteed; with income ceasing immediately upon her death; or with a guarantee of a refund, to a second beneficiary, of that portion of the principal yet unpaid. If the 5-, 10-, 15-, or 20-year guaranteed option is selected, it means that the recipient will be paid a specified income for the rest of her life. If she dies before the guaranteed period is up, a second beneficiary will continue to receive the monthly payments for the balance of the guaranteed period. For example, if a life income with "ten years certain," as it is called, has been selected and the recipient dies after receiving payments for

TABLE 4 FIXED AMOUNT OPTION

Amount of Insurance	*Desired Income*															
	$10		$15		$20		$25		$30		$40		$50		$60	
	Yrs.	Mos.	Yrs.	Mos.	Yrs.	Mos.	Yrs.	Mos.	Yrs.	Mos.	Yrs.	Mos.	Yrs.	Mos.	Yrs.	Mos.
$ 1,000	9	3	5	11	4	4	3	5	2	10	2	1	1	8	1	4
2,000	21	6	12	11	9	3	7	3	5	11	4	4	3	5	2	10
3,000			21	6	14	11	11	5	9	3	6	9	5	4	4	4
4,000					21	6	16	2	12	11	9	3	7	3	5	11
5,000							21	6	17	0	12	0	9	3	7	7
6,000									21	6	14	11	11	5	9	3
7,000											18	1	13	9	11	1
8,000											21	6	16	2	12	11
9,000													18	9	14	11
10,000													21	6	17	0
11,000															19	2
12,000															21	6
13,000																
14,000																
15,000																
16,000																
17,000																
18,000																
19,000																
20,000																
25,000																
30,000																
40,000																
50,000																

only two years, the company will continue the income to a designated beneficiary for another eight years. The longer the guaranteed period, the less the stipulated income.

The no refund option offers more income but provides for the cessation of all payments upon the death of the recipient. The installment refund option provides for the recipient to receive income for life. If her death occurs before the original death benefit has been paid, a secondary beneficiary will continue to receive the income until the full original proceeds have been paid out. Under a cash refund option, the secondary beneficiary will receive the balance of the death benefit in lump sum rather than income.

The values of these options should be quite obvious. The interest only option can, for example, be used to guarantee that an educational fund be available for your children and that, meanwhile, they derive income from the interest which this educational fund draws. This option is also useful if you wish your wife to be able to avail herself of all or part of the lump sum, but only when she is ready

Desired Income																			
$70		$75		$85		$100		$125		$150		$175		$200		$225		$250	
Yrs.	Mos.	Yrs.	Mos.	Yrs.	Mos.	Yrs.	Mos.	Yrs.	Mos.	Yrs.	Mos.	Yrs.	Mos.	Yrs.	Mos.	Yrs.	Mos.	Yrs.	Mos.
1	2	1	1		11		10		8		6		5		5		4		4
2	5	2	3	2	0	1	8	1	4	1	1		11		10		8		8
3	8	3	5	3	0	2	6	2	0	1	8	1	5	1	3	1	1	1	0
5	0	4	8	4	1	3	5	2	9	2	3	1	11	1	8	1	6	1	4
6	5	5	11	5	2	4	4	3	5	2	10	2	5	2	1	1	10	1	8
7	10	7	3	6	4	5	4	4	2	3	5	2	11	2	6	2	3	2	0
9	3	8	7	7	6	6	3	4	11	4	1	3	5	3	0	2	8	2	4
10	10	10	0	8	8	7	3	5	8	4	8	3	11	3	5	3	0	2	9
12	5	11	5	9	11	8	3	6	5	5	4	4	6	3	11	3	5	3	1
14	1	12	11	11	2	9	3	7	3	5	11	5	0	4	4	3	10	3	5
15	10	14	6	12	6	10	4	8	1	6	7	5	7	4	10	4	3	3	10
17	7	16	2	13	10	11	5	8	10	7	3	6	1	5	4	4	8	4	2
19	6	17	10	15	3	12	7	9	9	7	11	6	8	5	9	5	1	4	6
21	6	19	7	16	9	13	9	10	7	8	7	7	3	6	3	5	6	4	11
		21	6	18	3	14	11	11	5	9	3	7	10	6	9	5	11	5	4
				19	10	16	2	12	4	10	0	8	5	7	3	6	4	5	8
				21	6	17	5	13	3	10	9	9	0	7	9	6	10	6	1
						18	9	14	2	11	5	9	7	8	3	7	3	6	5
						20	1	15	2	12	2	10	2	8	9	7	8	6	10
						21	6	16	2	12	11	10	10	9	3	8	2	7	3
								21	6	17	0	14	1	12	0	10	6	9	3
										21	6	17	7	14	11	12	11	11	5
														21	6	18	5	16	2
																		21	6

to do so. While she is deciding how to utilize the money, she can be drawing interest on it.

Those options pertaining to a stipulated number of years of income or stipulated income as long as the money shall last can be extremely useful in planning for your children while they are in their minority. Thus, if you know that it requires at least $600 a month for your family to survive, you can place some of your insurance on an option calling for payment of that sum for as long as the money will last. If, on the other hand, you should wish to provide payment to your widow of a stipulated income during her years fifty-five to seventy, you can utilize the option which calls for payment over a 15-year period. This option also increases the over-all value of your policy. For example, a $25,000 policy used to provide income over a 15-year period will produce $166 per month. Multiplying these payments over a 15-year period, you will discover that, having used an income option, the total benefits received by your beneficiary amounts to $29,880. This is a 19.5 per cent increase over the original

$25,000 you left. The increase was effected at no charge to you or your beneficiary and contains the guaranteed guards against foolish investments which so many distraught widows and unbusinesslike wives need.

A question often arises related to the amount of insurance necessary to provide a certain income for a definite number of years. The chart below shows how much coverage you need for that purpose. It takes into consideration the fact that interest on any unused funds decreases the total amount necessary.

The life income options can mean the difference between starvation and survival to your wife. By putting a policy on a life income

TABLE 5 MONTHLY PAYMENTS FOR EACH $1000 OF PROCEEDS APPLIED

Age of Payee on Birthday Nearest Date of First Payment		*Life Income with Guaranteed Period*		*Life Income without Refund*	*Life Income with Cash Refund*
Male	*Female*	*10 Years*	*20 Years*		
36	40	3.33	3.29	3.34	3.24
37	41	3.37	3.33	3.38	3.27
38	42	3.42	3.38	3.43	3.32
39	43	3.48	3.42	3.49	3.36
40	44	3.53	3.47	3.54	3.40
41	45	3.59	3.52	3.60	3.45
42	46	3.65	3.57	3.67	3.49
43	47	3.71	3.62	3.73	3.54
44	48	3.78	3.67	3.80	3.59
45	49	3.84	3.73	3.87	3.65
46	50	3.91	3.78	3.95	3.70
47	51	3.99	3.84	4.03	3.76
48	52	4.07	3.90	4.11	3.82
49	53	4.15	3.96	4.20	3.88
50	54	4.23	4.02	4.29	3.95
51	55	4.32	4.08	4.39	4.02
52	56	4.41	4.15	4.49	4.09
53	57	4.51	4.21	4.60	4.16
54	58	4.60	4.28	4.71	4.24
55	59	4.71	4.34	4.83	4.32

TABLE 5 MONTHLY PAYMENTS FOR EACH $1000 OF PROCEEDS APPLIED—Continued

Age of Payee on Birthday Nearest Date of First Payment *		*Life Income with Guaranteed Period*		*Life Income without Refund*	*Life Income with Cash Refund*
Male	*Female*	*10 Years*	*20 Years*		
56	60	4.82	4.41	4.95	4.40
57	61	4.93	4.47	5.09	4.49
58	62	5.05	4.54	5.23	4.59
59	63	5.17	4.60	5.37	4.69
60	64	5.30	4.67	5.53	4.79
61	65	5.44	4.73	5.70	4.90
62	66	5.58	4.79	5.88	5.01
63	67	5.73	4.85	6.07	5.13
64	68	5.88	4.90	6.28	5.26
65	69	6.04	4.95	6.49	5.39
66	70	6.21	5.00	6.73	5.53
67	71	6.38	5.05	6.98	5.68
68	72	6.55	5.09	7.25	5.84
69	73	6.73	5.12	7.55	6.00
70	74	6.92	5.15	7.86	6.18
71	75	7.10	5.18	8.20	6.36
72	76	7.29	5.20	8.56	6.56
73	77	7.48	5.22	8.96	6.77
74	78	7.66	5.23	9.39	6.99
75	79	7.84	5.25	9.85	7.23
76	80	8.02	5.25	10.35	7.47
77	81	8.19	5.26	10.89	7.74
78	82	8.36	5.27	11.47	8.03
79	83 & over	8.51	5.27	12.11	8.32
80		8.65	5.27	12.81	8.65
81		8.78	5.27	13.56	8.99
82		8.89	5.27	14.38	9.35
83 & over		8.99	5.27	15.28	9.76

* Life Income options are not available below the ages shown.

TABLE 6 AMOUNT OF INSURANCE REQUIRED

Desired Monthly Income	*Number of Years*									
	1	2	3	4	5	6	7	8	9	10
$10										$1,063
15						$1,005	$1,158	$1,307	$1,453	1,595
20					$1,130	1,339	1,543	1,743	1,937	2,126
25				$1,144	1,412	1,674	1,929	2,178	2,421	2,658
30			$1,042	1,372	1,695	2,009	2,315	2,614	2,905	3,189
35			1,216	1,601	1,977	2,343	2,701	3,049	3,390	3,721
40			1,390	1,830	2,259	2,678	3,086	3,485	3,874	4,252
45		$1,055	1,563	2,058	2,542	3,013	3,472	3,920	4,358	4,784
50		1,172	1,737	2,287	2,824	3,347	3,858	4,356	4,842	5,315
55		1,290	1,911	2,516	3,106	3,682	4,244	4,792	5,326	5,847
60		1,407	2,084	2,744	3,389	4,017	4,629	5,227	5,810	6,378
65		1,524	2,258	2,973	3,671	4,352	5,015	5,663	6,294	6,910
70		1,641	2,432	3,202	3,953	4,686	5,401	6,098	6,779	7,441
75		1,758	2,605	3,430	4,236	5,021	5,787	6,534	7,263	7,973
80		1,876	2,779	3,659	4,518	5,356	6,172	6,969	7,747	8,504
85	$1,009	1,993	2,953	3,888	4,800	5,690	6,558	7,405	8,231	9,036
90	1,069	2,110	3,126	4,116	5,083	6,025	6,944	7,840	8,715	9,567
95	1,128	2,227	3,300	4,345	5,365	6,360	7,330	8,276	9,199	10,099
100	1,187	2,344	3,473	4,575	5,650	6,699	7,722	8,720	9,694	10,644
125	1,484	2,930	4,342	5,717	7,059	8,368	9,644	10,889	12,104	13,288
150	1,781	3,516	5,210	6,860	8,471	10,041	11,573	13,067	14,525	15,945
175	2,078	4,102	6,078	8,003	9,883	11,715	13,502	15,245	16,946	18,603
200	2,374	4,688	6,946	9,146	11,294	13,388	15,430	17,422	19,366	21,260
225	2,671	5,274	7,815	10,290	12,706	15,062	17,359	19,600	21,787	23,918
250	2,968	5,860	8,683	11,433	14,118	16,735	19,288	21,778	24,208	26,575
300	3,561	7,032	10,419	13,719	16,941	20,082	23,145	26,133	29,049	31,890

basis, you assure her of a fundamental income for as long as she may live regardless of economic conditions, of her abilities as an investor, of her physical or mental state of health, and of how long she lives or how soon she dies. No way has been devised by man to accomplish this purpose other than through the annuity, or life income, principle of life insurance.

The Internal Revenue Code gives special tax considerations to the recipients of monies under settlement options of life insurance policies.

Monies left under installment payments receive very favorable tax treatment. The amount of insurance is divided by the number of years the installments are to be paid. The resulting amount is the annual income your beneficiary can receive free of income taxes. Any amount over this allowable income your widow receives is considered taxable interest earnings. However, she is also allowed an annual exclusion of $1,000 a year. Thus, almost all the income your beneficiary will receive will be income tax free.

Number of Years											
11	12	13	14	15	16	17	18	19	20	21	25
$1,156	$1,246	$1,334	$1,420	$1,503	$1,585	$1,664	$1,742	$1,818	$1,892	$1,964	$2,234
1,734	1,869	2,001	2,129	2,255	2,377	2,496	2,613	2,726	2,837	2,945	3,351
2,311	2,492	2,667	2,839	3,006	3,169	3,328	3,484	3,635	3,783	3,927	4,468
2,889	3,114	3,334	3,549	3,758	3,962	4,160	4,354	4,544	4,728	4,908	5,585
3,467	3,737	4,001	4,258	4,509	4,754	4,992	5,225	5,452	5,674	5,890	6,702
4,045	4,360	4,668	4,968	5,261	5,546	5,824	6,096	6,361	6,619	6,871	7,819
4,622	4,983	5,334	5,678	6,012	6,338	6,656	6,967	7,270	7,565	7,853	8,936
5,200	5,606	6,001	6,387	6,764	7,131	7,488	7,838	8,178	8,510	8,834	10,053
5,778	6,228	6,668	7,097	7,515	7,923	8,320	8,708	9,087	9,456	9,816	11,169
6,356	6,851	7,335	7,807	8,266	8,715	9,152	9,579	9,996	10,402	10,798	12,286
6,933	7,474	8,001	8,516	9,018	9,507	9,984	10,450	10,904	11,347	11,779	13,403
7,511	8,097	8,668	9,226	9,769	10,300	10,816	11,321	11,813	12,293	12,761	14,520
8,089	8,720	9,335	9,936	10,521	11,092	11,648	12,192	12,722	13,238	13,742	15,637
8,667	9,342	10,002	10,645	11,272	11,884	12,480	13,062	13,630	14,184	14,724	16,754
9,244	9,965	10,668	11,355	12,025	12,676	13,312	13,933	14,539	15,129	15,705	17,871
9,822	10,588	11,335	12,065	12,775	13,469	14,144	14,804	15,448	16,075	16,687	18,988
10,400	11,211	12,002	12,774	13,527	14,261	14,976	15,675	16,356	17,020	17,668	20,105
10,978	11,834	12,669	13,484	14,278	15,053	15,808	16,546	17,265	17,966	18,650	21,222
11,571	12,475	13,358	14,118	15,058	15,877	16,677	17,456	18,217	18,959	19,683	22,408
14,444	15,570	16,669	17,742	18,787	19,807	20,800	21,770	22,717	23,639	24,539	27,923
17,333	18,684	20,003	21,290	22,544	23,768	24,960	26,124	27,260	28,367	29,447	33,507
20,222	21,798	23,337	24,838	26,301	27,729	29,120	30,478	31,803	33,095	34,365	39,092
23,110	24,912	26,670	28,386	30,058	31,690	33,280	34,832	30,346	37,822	39,262	44,676
25,999	28,026	30,004	31,935	33,816	35,652	37,440	39,186	40,890	42,550	44,170	50,261
28,888	31,140	33,338	35,483	37,573	39,613	41,600	43,540	45,433	47,278	49,078	55,845
34,665	37,368	40,005	42,579	45,087	47,535	49,920	52,248	54,519	56,733	58,893	67,014

For example, suppose you leave a $100,000 policy under option to pay your widow $11,500 a year for ten years. The total, $100,000, is divided by ten years, resulting in $10,000 a year which is the allowable tax-free income. In addition, the $1,000 exclusion is added to give your widow $11,000 of the $11,500 a year tax free. The balance of $500 is taxable income in her low tax bracket.

If your policy provides for life income, the same method of calculation is used except that the number of years by which the total is to be divided is determined by consulting government mortality tables for your wife's normal life expectancy. Only that amount received in excess of this calculation, less the widow's $1,000 exemption, is taxable.

If your policy is left to your widow at an interest only option, the total income received is pure interest and fully taxable. The widow's exclusion does not apply.

Besides the settlement options mentioned, there are other ways of settling a policy; these can be arranged with the consent of your company. Most companies will go along with any reasonable way of paying death proceeds.

It is important to know that once you have chosen a particular way of having the monies paid, this cannot be changed by the beneficiary unless you specifically instruct the company to permit such change. This can well become a double-edged sword. If your choice of unchangeable options is a bad one and special situations develop that make it impossible for your beneficiaries to survive on the terms and incomes that you have provided, nothing can be done to change these terms. Your beneficiary may find herself with plenty of money but no way to get to it. On the other hand, if you have permitted the company to allow changes by the beneficiary, the over-all plan that you have provided for the security of your family may be destroyed by a move of foolishness or compassion on the part of your widow, by bad advice, by unsafe investments, and by other unforeseeable actions. A combination of fixed income and interest only monies which can be tapped during an emergency may provide an answer to this dilemma.

You may utilize more than one option even in a single policy. For example, you may stipulate for the payment of a lump sum upon death, for a payment of monthly income until a certain date, and for a payment then of certain sums at certain times. To illustrate, if you own a $50,000 policy, you may ask that $10,000 be paid immediately upon death, that $32,000 be paid as monthly income until your child is eighteen years old, and that $2,000 be paid to that child each year over a four-year period for educational purposes.

Regardless of which of the settlement options you use, you will find that you have increased the death benefit considerably and have made the proceeds of the policy safer and more dependable for your family. You have, in effect, written an unbreakable will. Because of the earned interest involved, the use of settlement options often increases the death benefits as much as 40 per cent. Conversely, those who do not use settlement options sometimes force upon a widow lump sums which are quickly dissipated. Inevitably, many widows will find situations of chance or poor advice that will decrease these sums, resulting in financial loss. Money management is difficult enough. If there is a method of dependable money management that not only does not cost anything but also makes money for you, by all means make use of it.

13. *The Beneficiary*

Who Will Receive Your Money?

You can lose thousands of hard-earned dollars by an act of chivalry.

You can partially disinherit your children by an act of carelessness.

You can cause your family unnecessary hardship by an act of innocent ignorance.

When you designate a beneficiary in your policy, you are, in effect, writing a life insurance will. Great care must be taken that you direct the insurance company to pay the monies provided by your policies in a manner fulfilling your intentions.

There are two basic types of beneficiary designations:

IRREVOCABLE BENEFICIARY

Under such an arrangement, you cannot change beneficiaries, borrow on your policy, assign it as collateral, or cash it in without the written consent of your beneficiary. She has a vested interest in this family asset.

Sometimes, a young physician will elect an irrevocable designation to prove his confidence in his wife. She looks upon this act as an added measure of security and trust. However, one such physician paid many years of premiums, built up a sizable cash equity in his policy, and then found his marriage on the tragic road to divorce. He no longer wanted his wife to receive benefits after his death, but he was helpless. All he could do was to stop paying premiums. The values to which he was still entitled, such as cash equities or reduced death benefits, were lost to him. His estranged wife would eventually receive them.

Another physician encountered difficulties when his wife predeceased him. Her interest in his policies passed to her estate which was created for heirs in addition to himself. Some policies do stipulate that, in the event the beneficiary is the first to die, her interest shall automatically revert to the insured. But the doctor's policy did not contain this provision.

Practical reasons for an irrevocable beneficiary designation do exist. Even in those states that do not prohibit creditors from attaching a policy's value or equity, the vested interest of the beneficiary would prevent such take over were you ever to become bankrupt. Also, if you borrow money, one of the conditions imposed upon you by the lender may be the purchase of insurance in the amount of the loan, with the lender named as irrevocable beneficiary.

Approximately 4 per cent of all life insurance in force today contains an irrevocable beneficiary clause.

REVOCABLE BENEFICIARY

This method guarantees your complete control over the policy. You may change beneficiaries whenever you see fit to do so, borrow on your policy, assign it as collateral, or cash it in.

Many states protect your policies against creditors, if you become bankrupt, even when you reserve the right to change beneficiaries. No uniform rule exists, however. Statutes and court decisions vary from state to state.

Since the problem of attachment by creditors does not exist when your wife becomes an irrevocable beneficiary, you can designate her as such and assign the policy to her just before becoming insolvent. However, if you personally pay premiums after that, it may be recovered by your creditors.

About 96 per cent of all personal life insurance policies in force contain the right to change beneficiaries.

There are many methods of naming a beneficiary. Here are the ones most commonly used:

To Your Estate

If your policies are left to your estate, be sure that your will takes into consideration the fact that your family may experience undue delay in receiving the money while your estate is being settled by legal process. In many instances, this can cause unnecessary hardship. (Policies left to a named beneficiary do not have to go through probate, thus funds can become immediately available.)

In some states, special exemptions exist when monies are left to a named beneficiary rather than to the estate.

By naming your estate beneficiary, you may be making your policies subject to the claims of your creditors.

There are some advantages to naming your estate. You may, for example, desire an unusual distribution of your assets. This could be accomplished most conveniently by a will covering all your assets, including the sums derived from life insurance. You may be unmarried and wish to designate at least part of your life insurance for last expenses and burial purposes. The executor of your estate would find ready cash most helpful in disposing of these obligations.

To Your Wife and Children

Monies left to your wife as a named beneficiary do not become part of your estate for probate purposes. They are released directly by the insurance company without delay.

You can provide for your children to be secondary beneficiaries and to receive all unused benefits remaining after your wife's death.

In states that do not have a law regarding common disaster, you can stipulate that in the event you and your wife die simultaneously, she will be presumed to have died first and all monies will pass directly to your children. Some companies will permit you to stipulate that if your wife dies within a given number of days after your death, usually 30 days, the money will pass directly to your children without first becoming a part of your wife's estate.

Most insurance companies will go along with almost any reasonable designation. To carry out your intentions precisely, it is best for you to state your desires in simple and clear terms and request that the company's legal department devise the beneficiary designation. This service is rendered without charge by all companies. Before signing a company-prepared designation, read it carefully. Your desires may not have been understood clearly. It is safer to return the document for clarification or change than to risk the defeat of your desired objectives.

Keep in mind that the term "children" includes adopted children and those by a former marriage. It may be wise to either name each child individually, or to include the phrase "all children born of this marriage" if you wish to include future children automatically.

TO A TRUSTEE

You may wish to leave money to an individual or corporate trustee in order to fund a trust you have established for your wife and/or children. This method is often used when children, still in their minority, may inherit large sums. A corporate trustee can often serve as the children's property guardian most advantageously and with greatest flexibility. In this regard, legal advice is, of course, essential.

TO CREDITORS, CHARITIES, FRIENDS, RELATIVES, PARTNERS, CORPORATIONS

As previously stated, you can arrange to leave money to anyone you wish. All insurance companies will honor any reasonable, legal arrangement.

A proper beneficiary designation is essential in carrying out your intentions when you are no longer able to voice them. Remember to change these designations when circumstances, such as births or deaths in the family, necessitate a rearrangement of your insurance will.

All insurance companies render services in this regard without charge and at any time.

14. Should Your Wife Own Your Life Insurance?

You may effect a significant reduction in your gross estate with resultant savings on estate taxes if your wife owns your life insurance policies.

Suppose you carry a $100,000 policy on your life. When you die, this sum is included in your over-all estate before estate taxes are calculated. However, if this insurance on your life is owned by your wife, the $100,000 is not considered part of your estate. The possible reduction in federal estate taxes is obvious.

Before the 1954 Internal Revenue Code was devised, you could not transfer your policies to your wife unless:

1. You relinquished all rights of ownership, such as the rights to change beneficiaries, borrow, or assign benefits.
2. You gave away the policy forever. If there existed the slightest possibility that you might ever regain full or partial ownership, you were still considered owner.
3. You did not pay any further premiums yourself.

The 1954 Code eliminates the premium-paying provision. Today, you can transfer ownership of your policies to your wife, pay the premiums yourself, and still have the death benefits excluded from your estate.

You may have to pay some federal gift taxes when you make the transfer but, with the favorable exemptions available, these would usually be much lower than the federal estate tax that would be payable at your death if the policy remained as part of your estate.

If you die within three years of such transfer of policies, the insurance usually will be included in your gross estate. Any gift made within that time will be presumed to have been made in "contemplation of death" or with a view to escape estate taxes. Under that unfortunate circumstance, a transfer of policies will not have achieved your purpose.

Before you transfer ownership to your wife, consider these aspects:

1. You will give up all control of this asset. Your wife will be able to cash in your policies. It could prove to be dangerous if marital troubles ever developed.
2. You cannot avail yourself of the cash values for emergencies or opportunities without your wife's consent.
3. If your wife dies first, the value of the policies will be included in her estate, thus possibly creating a heretofore nonexistent estate tax problem for her estate.
4. The mood of Congress relating to the premium-paying test may change again in the future, and all your policies may once again be included in your estate. Of course, you would have achieved your objective had you died in the meantime and would, in the long run, be no worse or better off than you were before you made the transfer.
5. Some physicians assign their policies to their wives in order to put them beyond the reach of judgment creditors resulting from a possible malpractice suit.
6. If a purchase of new insurance is involved, your wife can apply for the coverage on your life, own all rights within the policy, and actually pay the premiums from her own funds. This would eliminate the possibility of congressional reinstatement of the premium-paying test in this instance.

Discuss your individual circumstances with your accountant and attorney before transferring forever your rights to a valuable form of property. Make absolutely certain that the advantages warrant such a move.

15. *Nonforfeiture Values*

What Happens When You Stop Paying On Your Life Insurance?

The insurance agent was sympathetic.

"Did he suffer much?" he asked.

"No, I guess not," the woman answered. "He just never woke up." She wept softly. "I really don't know what I'll do," she continued. "My husband carried a $20,000 policy for years and years. Then, when the business fell apart, he had to let it go. Last year he had his first heart attack and it was too late to get any new insurance. And now. . . ."

The agent's eyes suddenly sparkled with interest. "May I see the policy your husband dropped years ago?"

Without a word, the widow left the room and returned with the document.

The agent studied it thoughtfully. After a few minutes, he announced to a startled woman:

"You will have a check for $20,000 in your hands within ten days."

A time may come when circumstances will demand that you discontinue insurance premium payments. It may be because of financial reverses, unusual opportunities, or the fact that the original need for coverage no longer exists.

Assuming that you owned a permanent life insurance policy (as opposed to term coverage), where do you stand financially at that time?

All permanent policies have built-in provisions for just that situation. These are called "nonforfeiture" or "surrender" benefits.

To illustrate, let us examine the case of Dr. Benson, age fifty, who has owned a $10,000 whole life policy for 20 years.

Dr. Benson's children are happily married and financially secure. He now wishes to discontinue premium payments on that particular policy.

Dr. Benson has three choices:

Cash-In Option

He may cash in his policy for approximately $3,280 plus dividend accumulations, if any. The total premiums paid during the 20 years amount to about $4,000. He therefore gets approximately 82 per cent of his deposits back, plus dividends accumulated or received. However, he no longer has any coverage.

Paid-Up Insurance Option

He may exchange the policy for one with a smaller death coverage of approximately $5,380. No further premiums are required. Upon his death, his beneficiary will receive this sum which is about 33 per cent more than he has paid in. Any accumulated dividends can be withdrawn when this choice is made, permitted to accumulate for later use, or can be left with the company for the future benefit of the beneficiary.

Extended Coverage Option

He may request that the company extend his full $10,000 coverage for another 19½ years. If he dies during this period, the company will pay the full amount of the policy, even though no additional premiums have been paid. At the end of the 19½ years, the policy expires and the death benefit no longer exists. (Actually, the company has taken Dr. Benson's cash value and purchased 19½ years of term insurance for him.) A few companies will permit him to change his mind at a later date and convert his extended coverage back to the original policy by payment of back premiums with interest.

The figures used in this illustration will, of course, vary depending on the company, when the policy was purchased, your age, and other factors.

Which of these choices is the wisest?

That depends on your reason for wanting to discontinue the insurance, your health, your other assets, and on many additional factors.

Use the Cash-In Option If:

1. You no longer need the coverage, but need cash. (Remember, however, you can borrow, at interest, the same amount without having to surrender the policy.)
2. You can no longer afford the premiums and have no need for coverage.

Use the Paid-Up Insurance Option If:

1. You still need protection, but cannot afford future payments.
2. You are ready to retire and wish to keep a smaller amount of coverage and at the same time reduce your over-all expenditures to keep in line with a smaller retirement budget.

Use the Extended Coverage Option If:

1. You cannot afford further premiums, but need full coverage for a few more years.
2. You are in very poor health and don't expect to outlive the years this benefit will continue to cover you.

During the depression, many men had to discontinue premium payments. Some were not aware of these options and felt that their policies had no value. Since the extended benefit usually goes into effect automatically if no other choice is made, insurance companies, without the knowledge of their former policyholders, continued coverage on many thousands of people for many years. To this day, companies are holding uncollected millions for beneficiaries who are not aware of the fact that the policy their loved ones had cancelled years ago still provided value at their deaths.

Each policy, other than term insurance, contains a chart entitled "Nonforfeiture Provisions" which shows the exact cash, paid-up, and extended values for any given year. Look over your old lapsed life insurance policies. You may discover that although you are through with them, they are not through with you.

16. *Waiver of Premium*

THEY WILL PAY YOUR PREMIUMS

Recovery was slow. Dr. Benson wheeled his chair over to the sun-bathed window. It would probably be another year before he would be able to get out of that confounded contraption.

His wife brought a cheerful greeting and the morning mail. There was a letter from his insurance company. Dr. Benson opened it apprehensively. His yearly premium of $1,200 was due this month. He read, a smile of relief on his face, that the company was crediting his policy with an annual premium of $1,200 in accordance with the provisions of the waiver of premium clause, and they hoped for his very speedy recovery.

For a small additional cost, you can add a disability provision, known as waiver of premium, to your life insurance policy. Many companies automatically incorporate this benefit into their premiums for all policies. The waiver of premium provides that in the event of your total and permanent disability, the company will waive all premiums as long as the disability lasts. Figuratively speaking, the company will pay the premiums for you. All cash values and dividends continue to accrue as if you were still sending in your checks. If and when you recover, you do not have to pay back any deposits credited to you by the company.

At first thought, you might marvel at so fine a benefit at so little a cost. But there is reason for the slight cost. The risk to the company is minimized by the following restrictions:

1. Benefits do not begin until you have been disabled for six months, but then the assumption of the premium obligation by the

company is usually retroactive to the beginning of the disability. Any premium paid during that period is refunded.

2. You must be so disabled as to be unable to engage in any work for profit or remuneration.

3. Disability must render you unable to earn money in any capacity.

4. Disabilities due to war, military service, aviation, poison, gas, suicide attempts, participation in riots or insurrections, attempts to commit assault or felony, civil commotion, or participation in a strike are usually excluded from coverage. All companies use some or all of these restrictions in the waiver of premium clause.

5. The benefit usually expires at age sixty for males and age fifty-five for females—when each approaches the threshold of greatest risk of disability.

It would seem that these limitations make the waiver of premium a poor buy. However, this is not the case. Despite these limitations, you are wise to purchase waiver of premium on all policies. As a matter of fact, if your present ones do not have this benefit, you should have it added. The cost is certainly small enough to make it worthwhile. At least you will know that if misfortune strikes you, which automatically increases the possibility of a premature death, you will not lose your coverage due to an inability to pay premiums.

Furthermore, your cash values are increasing even while you are disabled and stand ready as an ever-appreciating emergency fund. Your premium is waived as it comes due. If you pay annually, it will be waived, after six months of disability, for the entire next year. If, however, you pay premiums quarterly, it will be waived for only three months, and then again for three months if you are still disabled, and so on until you recover. The annual premium method, therefore, makes the waiver of premium clause more valuable. Even if you recover in the seventh month of disability, your full annual premium will have been waived had it fallen due while you were disabled.

Check your policies and make sure the waiver of premium benefits are included.

17. *Disability Riders with Life Insurance*

A Relic of the Past

"I don't need disability income policies," Dr. Benson insisted. "All my life insurance policies have disability riders. They're much cheaper that way because it's a package deal, you know."

The agent smiled: "They're cheaper all right, Doctor. Please permit me to give you the facts."

Many companies are once again offering disability income riders that can be attached to a life insurance policy. Before the depression, these riders were common. During this period of economic drought, when many men could "earn" more by being disabled than by working, fraudulent and often brilliant schemes caused such great losses that most companies discontinued these benefits on new policies.

Disability income riders usually provide a monthly income of $10 per $1,000 of life insurance carried. This income is payable to your age sixty-five, at which time your life policy matures for its face value. For example, if you had a $25,000 whole life policy and were permanently disabled, you would receive $250 per month to age sixty-five and then $25,000 in cash, or as much life income as this cash would purchase. If you accepted the lump sum, you would no longer have a death benefit. If you accepted income, your beneficiaries would be entitled to that portion of income, if any, which is guaranteed in the event of your early death.

The cost of the disability income rider is approximately 30 per cent of your basic life insurance premium.

Is this rider a good buy? NO.

In the last 20 years, the insurance industry has devised so many fine noncancellable disability policies as to make this rider as outdated as the midwife. Although the premium charged for these quality policies is higher than that charged for the rider, the extra investment represents a bargain.

Let us analyze the basic provisions of the disability income rider in life insurance:

1. You are considered disabled only if you are unable to engage in any occupation whatsoever for gain or profit. This definition of disability is the most glaring weakness of the rider. You must be a living vegetable before you can receive benefits. With quality disability policies, however, you can receive income if you are unable to do the duties of your own profession.

2. Payments do not begin until you have been disabled for six months. Since separate disability policies are available with benefits beginning as early as the first day for accidents, and the eighth day for sicknesses, the rider may lose its practicality due to the long waiting period.

3. You cannot get the rider if you are older than age fifty and, regardless of when you obtained it, the benefit expires at age fifty-five, the period of greatest risk. Separate disability policies can be purchased at older ages and, in all instances, can provide coverage to at least retirement age sixty-five.

4. You must maintain your life insurance policy to keep your disability rider. If circumstances demand that you decrease your over-all life insurance program, this requirement can force you to either keep policies you no longer need nor want, or to lose disability benefits you may never again be able to replace.

5. You lose your disability rider if you ever decide to change your policy to a paid-up contract in a smaller amount, or if you place the policy under the extended insurance benefits which continue death protection only for a number of years.*

6. When you are sixty-five, your life insurance policy automatically matures for a cash payment. In some instances, this may be a distinct advantage due to the fact that it provides an opportunity for

* See Chapter 15, "Nonforfeiture Values—What Happens When You Stop Paying On Your Life Insurance."

income while you are still disabled; in other instances, however, it is a disadvantage since it leaves no death benefit to that beneficiary for whose protection you purchased the policy originally. Although you can leave the lump sum with the insurance company until you die, the temptation to avail yourself of ready cash is almost impossible to conquer.

7. With few companies can you obtain more than $300 per month income under the rider. This is undoubtedly insufficient at today's living cost. Yet, ownership of this amount of relatively limited coverage will influence your ability to purchase quality disability policies.*

These seven points should be sufficient to discourage your future purchase of such a rider. Let your life insurance protect your family's future in the event of premature death, and let a quality noncancellable disability income policy replace your earnings during your disability. Contracts are available today to suit almost any need and situation, including yours.

* See Chapter 44, "Issue and Participation Limits—There Is a Limit to How Much You Can Buy."

18. *Accidental Death and Dismemberment*

Double Your Money If You Die Our Way!

Dr. Benson had fallen asleep on the beach. It was a sleep of exhaustion. He was totally unaware of the intensity of the sunlight that beat down upon him.

Several hours later, a bather called the police emergency squad. Dr. Benson never emerged from the coma. He died on the way to the hospital.

Two weeks later the widow, Eleanore Benson, received another shock. The insurance company informed her that they were sending her a check for the amount of the doctor's life insurance policy, but that they were denying any additional benefits under the accidental death provision since death by heat or sunstroke was specifically excluded.

With the exception of decreasing term insurance, almost all policies make available a provision whereby the company will pay double the amount contracted for in the event that the death occurs because of an accident. Recently, some companies have stipulated that they will pay triple the amount if such accident occurs on a common carrier such as a bus, train, or plane, under stated conditions.

The cost for the accidental death benefit is relatively small; yet, it may not be wise to purchase it. Your needs do not necessarily change or increase because your death happens to be accidental. Furthermore, almost all accidental death benefits are worded in such a manner as to limit the liability of the company. For example, most of these provisions mention "death by accidental means." This phraseology limits the liability of the company to those deaths occurring by a type of accident to which you made no contributory actions whatever. In other words, the cause as well as the result of the accident becomes very important. If, for instance, you choke to death while on a picnic, it can be said that, by eating, you contributed to your own death. However, if while you are picnicking, a tree falls on you, this is considered accidental means. Some companies use the term "accidental injury." Under this terminology, only the results are considered, but not the causes. Any accidental death is then considered as being covered.

All companies have certain exclusions in their accidental death clauses. The most common ones are: suicide regardless of whether the insured is sane or insane; the taking of poison or gas; illness, physical or mental infirmity; any aviation other than if you are a fare-paying passenger on a regular airline; war or military service.

Many companies also have some combination of the following exclusions: death by insanity, heat or sunstroke; as a result of medical treatment, surgical operation, or anesthetics; from drugs or sedatives; as a result of committing or attempting to commit assault or felony, violation of the law, insurrection or riot; from intentional injuries inflicted by another; from engagement in an illegal occupation; while under the influence of intoxicants or narcotics; while a civilian in time of war, or, while engaged in an occupation involving association with military or naval operations.

The purchase of accidental death benefits does not materially influence your basic insurance program. It is entirely a matter of personal choice. Some men buy it on the chance that if they are killed accidentally and in accordance with their policies' provisions, their families will be so much better off. Others purchase this benefit because they feel that their basic programs are not adequate and, in the event of accidental death, the additional monies might more properly provide for their families.

Accidental death benefits should be bought under those circumstances. However, its limitations must be thoroughly understood so that you will not falsely depend on its benefits.

Some companies also have special dismemberment clauses in some of their policies. These usually refer to the loss of a hand at, or above, the wrist; a foot at, or above, the ankle; or, the irrevocable loss of sight. In most instances, a loss of this nature provides for a lump sum to be paid to you. Since the occurrence of such a loss is extremely rare, most companies writing these benefits do not charge special premiums for them.

Dismemberment and double-dismemberment clauses cannot, of course, hurt you. On the other hand, the inclusion or exclusion of these should not unduly influence you in any way when you purchase a life insurance policy.

19. *Special Riders*

Extras For Sale

Dr. Benson was very much concerned about his children. They were only babies. He wanted to provide enough income in his estate for their sustenance until they were at least out of college.

He jotted down some figures:

Minimum needed to live:	$6,000 *a year*
Years until John is age 24 (1982)	20
Total insurance needed:	$120,000

From previous experience, Dr. Benson knew he could not, at this time, afford the premium required to purchase an additional $120,000 of coverage.

His agent had the answer. "Add a family income rider to one of your policies, Doctor," he advised, "and have it provide $6,000 a year from the date of your death until 1982."

Many companies permit special provisions to be added to their basic contracts. In all instances, these are designed to fill specific needs that you might have. There is a charge for each one, based on actuarial calculations. The use of some of these special riders and provisions can greatly enhance your personal insurance program and can also fill unusual needs peculiar to your own situation.

A word of caution is necessary. Use special riders only if you actually need their benefits. Very often the appeal of the unusual may cause you to lose sight of this.

Let us discuss some of these special provisions. (Not all companies have all of these.)

MORTGAGE PROTECTION RIDER

This rider provides for the payment in full of the balance of your mortgage, in the event you die during the mortgage-paying period. This is a form of decreasing term insurance.*

RETURN OF CASH VALUE RIDER

An ever-increasing number of companies will include a provision that calls for an additional death benefit, in the amount of the cash value of the policy, up to age sixty-five. For example, a $50,000 whole life policy with this rider, taken out at age thirty-five, would provide a death benefit of $68,550 in its twentieth year. This is made up of the $50,000 value of the policy plus an additional death benefit of $18,550, which is the exact cash value that this policy has acquired. This provision is usually used in that type of a program from which you withdraw and borrow the cash value each year in order to pay the premium.† With this rider, the death benefit therefore remains constant even though you have borrowed the cash value which normally would be deducted at time of death.

RETURN OF PREMIUM RIDER

Some companies will provide that, in the event of your death during the first 20 years of the life of the policy, they will pay not only the death benefits, but will also return all premiums paid in. At age thirty-five, the additional charge for this benefit is approximately 9 per cent of the total premium. This rider attains its greatest value from the fifteenth to the twentieth years of policy ownership. Prior to those years, it is not a very good buy since, for the premium charged for it, you can undoubtedly obtain a greater amount of term insurance for use as additional protection.

* See Chapter 7, "Types of Policies—The Tools of the Trade."
† See Chapter 33, "Bank Funding–Minimum Deposit Plan—The Tax Gimmick."

Payor Benefit Rider

Because estate planners, attorneys, and accountants have made the professional man more aware of the necessity of owning life insurance on his wife, several insurance companies have issued a benefit which provides that, in the event of your disability or death, those premiums which you were paying for your wife's life insurance be waived and that no further premiums need be paid. This benefit can be most useful if circumstances demand that your wife be substantially insured. Assuming, for example, that the premium on your wife's policy is $500 per year, it may, without this benefit, create a hardship for your wife to carry on her own policy at that premium rate. With this benefit, however, the wife's policy is paid-up and there is no need for her to pay further premiums.

The payor benefit rider is widely available with most policies insuring the lives of children.

Increasing Term Rider

This provision adds additional death benefits to an existing policy at specific and predetermined amounts over a period of years. The premium you pay for it remains level. The increasing amount of coverage usually may be converted to any form of permanent coverage at any time without evidence of insurability. This makes the benefit extremely useful in matters of business or partnership insurance. For example, if a professional partnership wishes to insure, over a ten-year-period, for the eventual increase in the value of the partnership, this may be an excellent way of accomplishing that goal. Very often partners are reluctant to own more coverage than is actually necessary at the time the insurance is purchased; yet, they may find themselves unable, from a health point of view, to obtain additional coverage as the partnership grows. The increasing term benefit may be the answer.

Family Income Rider

Basically, this provision guarantees the family a definite income for a definite period of time, starting with the date of purchase of the coverage, in addition to any other benefits.* It is used primarily to provide enough income while your children are in their minority.

FAMILY MAINTENANCE RIDER

This provision adds a definite amount of money for a definite period of time. For example, it could provide $50,000 of additional coverage for a 20-year-period. Should you die at any time during those 20 years, the family will receive the $50,000. At the end of the 20 years, the extra protection expires. Technically, this is known as a level term rider.*

INTERIM TERM RIDER

One of the least known and yet most useful term riders available, the interim term rider enables you to apply for a permanent life insurance policy, put the death benefit into immediate effect, but postpone regular premium payments (usually up to six months), to a more convenient date. For example, you may wish to own a $20,000 whole life policy but, because of an impending tax deadline, you may wish to postpone regular premium payments for four months. Have your policy issued with four months of interim term. For a single payment of approximately $60 at age thirty-five, the policy will be in effect, insofar as death benefits are concerned, for four months. Then the whole life policy automatically becomes effective at the regular premium rate.

It is important to emphasize, once again, that you should not add riders solely because they are novel. Sometimes the benefit of a rider in a particular situation is not justified by its cost.

* See Chapter 7, "Types of Policies—The Tools of the Trade."

20. *Your Insurability*

Pay Now—Buy Later

Young Dr. Benson had left instructions with his aide to turn away any insurance man who called or came to the office. He had even successfully evaded several of his former classmates who had become insurance agents. He had too many other matters to consider and intended to wait until his practice enlarged before undertaking any additional policy purchases.

Now, with a baby on the way, Dr. Benson was ready to increase his life insurance program. He made a mental note to ask a few of his colleagues for recommendations to good agents.

One morning, Dr. Benson found it difficult to remove his wedding band due to a slight swelling of his ring finger. Several days later, he felt feverish. He became aware of a difficulty in moving his hands. Dr. Benson was alarmed. Laboratory tests confirmed his fears—rheumatoid arthritis.

Dr. Benson had become uninsurable—at least he would never again be able to purchase a policy at a standard premium.

Life insurance is one commodity that cannot be purchased with money alone. You must qualify for each policy; you must prove that you are in good health at the time of purchase. Most doctors establish an insurance program gradually over a period of years. They may start with a small policy during the lean years, then purchase additional policies as their needs and income grow. Eventually, they build programs that they feel are adequate for family protection and for other estate purposes. However, some doctors find, with consternation, that they have become uninsurable before they have been able to complete their programs.

When they could have qualified for insurance, they did not need the coverage, nor were they able to afford it. When they needed and could afford it, they could not qualify for it.

There are two ways in which you can guarantee yourself future ownership of life insurance.

You can purchase a large amount of term insurance, giving you the right to convert all or portions of it over a period of years, regardless of your state of health. This method also provides an immediate death benefit in the amount of the term insurance purchased.

If, however, you have little need for large death benefits at this time, you should consider the relatively new concept of guaranteed insurability provided by a rider to a basic policy.

Here is how this new concept works:

Suppose you purchased a $10,000 whole life policy. For a small additional premium (from $15 to $25 a year, depending on your age), most insurance companies would include a provision guarantying you the right to purchase another $10,000 of coverage without medical examination every three years beginning with age twenty-five and ending with age forty. At those times, you could obtain any permanent (not term) policies issued by the company. You would pay the standard premiums charged for the plans at those ages.

For example, if you are thirty years old now and purchase a $10,000 policy with guaranteed insurability rider, you will be able to purchase another $10,000 policy four more times, at ages thirty-one, thirty-four, thirty-seven, and forty. Thus, your original purchase assures you of a total of $50,000 of coverage by the time you are forty. Naturally, if you want more coverage, you can obtain it if you can qualify physically. Conversely, if you do not want more coverage at the purchase option dates, you can forego your options. But at least $50,000 is guaranteed, no matter what your state of health may be. For the young doctor, this is a way of increasing his insurance program as his needs and earning abilities increase, regardless of his state of health. It keeps pace with his growth.

The older doctor should consider this rider for his sons. A $10,000 policy will assure the youngsters of up to a total of $70,000 by the time they reach age forty. In later years, this may be invaluable to them.

It has always been said that insurance can only be purchased when you don't need it. The guaranteed insurability rider now makes this statement invalid.

The only thing worse than being hounded by insurance agents is being given up by them as a lost cause.

21. *The Special Risk*

Do you own a "rated" policy? Do you pay an additional premium because of an unfavorable health history? Do you have a disability policy which excludes certain ailments or diseases?

Thousands of physicians have paid extra premiums or have owned limited disability policies for years because of a condition existing at the time they applied for the insurance. Many have since been cured or at least have had no recurrences. Because of medical research and good claim experience, insurance companies have assumed a more liberal attitude in the last decade toward illness considered dangerous years ago. Medical science has made great strides in procedures and treatment.

You have the right to request the removal or reduction of a rating from your policy. Insurance companies are usually willing to reconsider. In many instances, you will have your rating removed without hesitation. The original reason for it may have vanished a long time ago. On the other hand, the company may request a medical examination at your own expense before considering a removal of rating. Based on the results of such examination, your request may be granted or the rating may be reduced.

In any event, an attempt by you to have a rating removed or reduced will result in one of the following:

1. Lower premiums—achieved by removal or reduction of extra charges (some companies will even return premiums retroactively).

2. Broader coverage—by removal or rewording of restrictions in your disability policy.

3. Clearer position—your company, although refusing your request, will usually indicate if and when it will consider another request more favorably.

Under no circumstances can you be penalized for trying. Even if it is determined that your health has deteriorated, the insurance company cannot, by law, place further restrictions on your policy or charge an even higher premium.

If you are successful in having ratings completely removed, you will be able to purchase new insurance at standard prices and your permanent records with the insurance companies will classify you as a good risk.

After one company has granted your request, the other companies usually fall into line. As a matter of fact, your success with one is a powerful persuader with others.

The underwriters of an insurance company, comfortably seated at a desk hundreds or thousands of miles away, cannot be aware of your improved health status unless you take action. Your agent or local company office has the required forms.

You have absolutely nothing to lose. But, you must make the first move.

22. *The Change of Plan Clause*

You Can Change Your Policy

The majestic, stoic, and steadfast Empire State Building, tallest building in the world, was so constructed as to sway under extreme wind pressures. During a gale of 102 miles per hour, the building bends almost 3 inches. Without this measure of elasticity, the building would long ago have crumbled.

A good life insurance policy should also provide for flexibility. This should include your contractual right to change the type of policy from one to another as your needs change.

Most companies will permit changes as a matter of convenience to you but not on a contractual basis, especially if they do not effect an increase in risk. Others include a change of plan clause in their policies, thus making the flexibility guaranteed.

You may change your policy in one of two ways.

From a Lower Premium Type to a Higher One

For example, you may want a whole life policy changed to retirement income after your children are self-supporting. This can be accomplished by paying the difference in cash values between the two policies plus interest of from 3 to 5 per cent on that sum, depending on the company. No medical examination is required since there is no increase in risk to the company. As a matter of fact, you are paying more for the same risk. You must deposit the difference in values because you are changing to a policy that guarantees a higher cash equity. The interest is necessary to compensate for the additional interest your larger premiums would have earned.

When converting in this manner, you receive a policy which is dated as of the younger age when you first took out the original policy. This means not only a lower future premium but, if your policy contains a change of plan clause, it often means the preservation of more favorable retirement benefits available in old policies.

When should you convert to a higher premium policy?

Let us say you have owned a $50,000 whole life policy for many years. You are now nearing retirement age. Your outside investments have appreciated. Now you wish to liquidate some of these in order to obtain income that you cannot outlive. You might purchase an annuity. On the other hand, you may decide to convert your $50,000 whole life policy by investing in its cash value. You would then obtain the annuity guarantees of your old policy, which are higher than any you could obtain today or will be able to obtain in the future.

Another reason for changing to a higher equity policy such as retirement income may be that you may wish to increase the savings element of your insurance, when your income permits such increase, as one aspect in your preparation for retirement.

Whenever you plan to convert to a higher premium policy, it is usually most advantageous to use that policy which has the highest retirement guarantees. It is usually an older one.

Although most companies will permit changes by company practice, a change of plan clause guarantying this right and outlining the conditions can be of great value to you in future years.

From a Higher Premium Type to a Lower One

You may, for example, own high-cost policies which have comparatively low death benefits. Your needs may now dictate more protection. Your finances may not permit the purchase of additional coverage. A conversion of your policies would lower your premiums sufficiently to permit you to invest the difference in additional protection.

When you make this change, you are increasing the risk to the company that holds your high-equity policy. Although the amount of coverage does not change, the company is receiving less premium for it; or, if you purchase additional insurance, you will receive much more coverage for the premium you used to pay. Therefore, you must prove to the company that you are still insurable when such a change is made. This usually means a medical examination. If you pass the examination, the change is granted. If you do not qualify, the conversion is not granted. A few companies will permit a downward change under certain conditions without evidence of insurability.

Assuming that the change is made, you will receive a policy dated as of the original younger age. You will also receive the difference in cash equity between the old policy, which has built up a high reserve, and the new one which, had it been purchased in its present form originally, would have built up a smaller reserve by this time. The monies that are released can be taken in cash, can be used to prepay the converted policy, or can be utilized to purchase additional coverage.

Again, this change is usually permitted by company practice. It is your guaranteed right in some policies, which include a change of plan clause, to change to a lower premium plan if you are insurable.

Since it is much easier to convert a low-cost into a higher-cost plan and, since the basic purpose of insurance—protection—can best be achieved with whole life or similar low-cost policies, why not build your program with such coverages and change at a latter date when the need for substantial retirement planning supercedes your need for family survival?

The following companies are among those that have change of plan clauses providing guarantees for changes to both higher and lower premium plans: *

Bankers, Iowa
Fidelity Mutual
Indianapolis Life
Mutual Benefit, N. J.
National Life & Acc.
Occidental, Calif.
Shenandoah Life
Continental American
Guardian Life of America
Metropolitan Life
National Fidelity
New England Life
Security Mutual, N. Y.

The following companies are among those that have limited provisions for change of plan, mostly from lower to higher premium plans:

* From *Who Writes What*—1961 Edition, published by The National Underwriter Company, 420 East Fourth St., Cincinnati 2, Ohio.

Acacia Mutual
Berkshire Life
Columbus Mutual
Connecticut Mutual
Great Southern Life
Intercoast Life
John Hancock
Lincoln National
Midland Mutual
National Life, Vt.
Pilot Life
Southland Life
Union Central

American National, Tex.
Business Men's Assurance
Companion Life
Great American Reserve
Guarantee Mutual Life
Life of Georgia
Massachusetts Mutual
Minnesota Mutual
Nationwide Insurance Co.
Provident Life & Accident
Southwestern Life
State Mutual of America
United Life & Accident

23. *Dividends*

Use Dividends to Best Advantage

Dr. Benson was ready to retire. Only one question remained unanswered: How much life income could he expect from his insurance policies? He called his agent who promised him a written report.

A few days later, Dr. Benson received the following breakdown:

Policy No.	*12569*	*38520*	*57210*	*Totals*
Cash Value	$17,790	$22,400	$15,540	$55,730
Accumulated Dividends	13,260	14,520	8,700	36,480
Total Value	31,050	36,920	24,240	92,210
Monthly Life Income from Cash Value	106	135	94	335
Monthly Life Income from Div.	80	88	53	221
Total Monthly Life Income (10 yrs. Guaranteed)	186	223	147	556

He was pleasantly surprised to find that his dividends, accumulated over the years, amounted to the healthy sum of $36,480. This increased his retirement income by $221 a month for as long as he would live. It would take a capital investment of $66,300 at 4 per cent after taxes to produce the same $221 a month.

Mutual life insurance companies pay dividends. The overwhelming majority of policies written in the United States are dividend-paying contracts. Unfortunately, the word "dividend" is a misnomer.

Dividends are a refund of overcharges made in your basic premium. Although they indirectly reflect the successful earnings and management of a company, they are still a return of your own money. That is one of the reasons why so-called dividends from your life insurance policy are not considered income for tax purposes. For the sake of safety, insurance companies have constructed their premium calculations so as to charge more than is actually necessary. At the end of each year, after all factors of mortality, investments, expenses, reserves, and other items have been considered, mutual companies usually find themselves with additional monies that really have not been needed. These monies are then returned to you, the policyholder, in proportion and relation to the policy you own, and are called dividends.

Dividends can be used in several ways:

1. They can be obtained in cash. Each year that a dividend is declared you will receive a check in the amount of the dividend. You can utilize this check in any way you desire.

2. Dividends can be used to reduce premiums. If you select this method, the company will deduct the amount of the dividends from your next premium, and you may then send a check for the difference.

3. Dividends may be left with the insurance company to accumulate at a minimum rate of interest, usually 2.5 per cent. At present, almost all companies are paying a higher percentage. The guaranteed percentage mentioned in the policy itself only indicates the amount below which the company can never go. Accumulated dividends are available to you, similar to a separate bank account, at any time without charge. Although the dividend is tax-exempt (since it is a refund of your own money), the interest earned on it is taxable. Accumulated dividends can greatly enhance the lump sum or retirement income available at retirement time. Should you die while dividends have accumulated, these accumulations go to your beneficiaries as an addition to the death benefit of the policy.

4. Dividends can be used to purchase paid-up insurance. Under this option, each time you receive a cash dividend, the company will automatically purchase the amount of death coverage that can be bought for that particular sum of cash. For example, a $50 dividend received at age thirty-five would purchase $110 of paid-up death benefit. Over a long period of years, these paid-up benefits can add a substantial amount to the death benefit of your insurance

program. They always remain yours, even if you ever find it necessary to discontinue the basic policy which originally earned them. For example, if a $20,000 whole life policy has built paid-up additional insurance of $5,000 over a period of years and you find it necessary to discontinue the $20,000 base policy, you will still have $5,000 of paid-up insurance for as long as you live. These paid-up benefits, similar to separate little insurance policies, also have guaranteed cash values. In that way, if you have reached retirement age and are ready to utilize your basic policy for retirement income purposes, you can also convert your paid-up coverage into cash to be paid to you as additional life income.

5. Yearly term insurance can be obtained instead of cash dividends. This option, called the fifth dividend option, is a relatively new and, so far, rare one. Each time a dividend is declared, the insurance company automatically purchases term insurance with it for one year. Since yearly term is extremely inexpensive especially at the younger ages, this option purchases tremendous additional coverage for relatively little money and can "beef up" your insurance when you need it most. For example, a $10 dividend received at age thirty-five would increase the death benefit of the policy throughout the next year by $2,230. At the end of each year, the term insurance purchased in this manner expires and new term insurance is automatically purchased by the new dividend without medical examination. Obviously, since the risk is much greater at the older ages, and the cost of even yearly term insurance increases greatly at old ages, the fifth dividend option will purchase a lesser amount of additional yearly coverage as you get older. On the other hand, the older you get, the less need you might have of additional coverage. Most companies will permit all or some conversion of this additional yearly protection to other forms of permanent insurance. In a way then, it can also become a device to protect future insurability. This particular point must be checked into carefully, since company practices differ. Usually, you must select the option when you first apply for the policy. You cannot change over to it at a later date. However, most companies will permit a change from the fifth dividend option to another option since you decrease their risk by such a change.

The companies listed below are among those offering the fifth dividend option:*

American Life, Conn.	American Life, Del.
American United	Bankers, Neb.
Berkshire Life	Confederation Life
Connecticut Mutual	Continental American
Eastern Life	Equitable, N. Y.
General American	Guardian Life of America
Home Life, N. Y.	Indianapolis Life
Jefferson Standard	Lincoln National
Manufacturers	Massachusetts Mutual
Mutual Benefit, N. J.	Mutual of New York
National Life, Vt.	New York Life
North American, Canada	Pacific Mutual
Penn Mutual	Phoenix Mutual
Pilot Life	Security Life & Accident
Security Mutual, N. Y.	Shenandoah Life
Union Mutual	United Life & Accident
United States Life	West Coast Life

Intelligent use of your dividends can have a great impact. Here are some examples of how dividends can influence your future security.

1. Although it is theoretically designed for you to pay premiums as long as you live, a whole life policy can be made fully paid-up for its full death benefit by the use of dividends. If you do not withdraw your dividends, a point will be reached at which the reserves of your policy plus the dividends will amount to enough to make your whole life policy fully paid-up. For example, a whole life policy purchased at age thirty-five may be paid-up in 26 years by the use of dividends.

2. Dividends can make a whole life policy mature into an endowment for retirement purposes. All companies provide that when the guaranteed cash values of the policy plus the accumulated dividends equal its face amount or death benefit, the contract has ma-

* From *Who Writes What*—1961 Edition, published by The National Underwriter Company, 420 East Fourth St., Cincinnati 2, Ohio.

tured and literally becomes an endowment. Thus, a $50,000 whole life policy taken out at age thirty-five will mature in 32 years for the full $50,000, at which time this total sum can be used for retirement income or can be withdrawn in cash.

3. Dividends are a separate little bank account which you can withdraw at any time without penalty or interest charge. If you ever find yourself in a position where you need money quickly, your dividend account can be of tremendous assistance.

4. Accumulated dividends can often serve as a college fund for your children.

5. Many companies will permit you to withdraw dividends and then replace them within a certain period of time at no penalty. Thus, instead of obtaining a short-term loan elsewhere at interest, some companies will allow you to withdraw your dividends, hold them for the length of time permitted, and then return the money without penalty or interest.

6. You can use the accumulated dividends from one policy to pay for an additional policy. Suppose you have $6,000 in dividends. You can purchase a new policy requiring, let us say, $800 a year in premiums, and pay this policy for seven and a half years in advance. During that time, your old and new policies will accumulate enough dividends to pay more advance premiums when the next due date arrives. Continuing for years, this method can give you additional protection without further outlay. The cash value which the new policy builds compensates for the withdrawal of equity from the old one.

Remember, however, that dividends are never guaranteed nor are any dividend promises ever anything other than a hope based on past performance. Needless to say, during the depression dividends were not what it was hoped they would be. In the last few years, however, most companies have steadily increased their dividends and have paid more than the guaranteed interest rate on those left to accumulate. Insurance companies are required by law to note on all printed matter that dividends are only estimates and not guarantees. Long-term projections as to their future value must, therefore, be considered as possible, but not necessarily probable.

Many policies also provide for one or both of the following dividends:

1. Postmortem dividends are additional dividends paid upon the death of the insured. They represent a pro-rata share of the dividend he would have received had he lived out the full year.

2. Termination dividends are paid by some companies when the policy is terminated either by maturity, death, surrender, or lapse if that policy has been in force for a certain required length of time.

Not all companies issue these dividends. You ought to know if yours does.

Dividends come from three sources:

Savings in Mortality

Usually the death claims experience of a company is less than that shown on the mortality table. These savings constitute a source of surplus to the company. They are returned to you in the form of a dividend.

Minimum Interest Rate the Company Anticipates Earning

This is usually estimated very conservatively. If a company's investment department has done its job well, and if the over-all earnings from investments in the economy are relatively high, the actual percentage earned on these investments usually exceeds the expected percentage. That difference constitutes another source of surplus for the company, returnable to you as a dividend.

Expense Loading

An insurance company expects a certain amount to be spent on operating expense. Through efficiency of management and other contributing factors, the company may be able to keep its expenses below the expected amount. That is another source of surplus reflected in your dividends.

All these sums that are left after all the liabilities of a company have been deducted from its total assets form a surplus fund from which the dividends you receive are paid.

How should you take your dividends?

In Cash, If:

1. You wish to use it as a premium payment on another policy.
2. You intend to make a gift of small sums such as at Christmas time.
3. Because of your high tax bracket, you want to avoid drawing interest on accumulated dividends. (Cash dividends are not taxed, but the interest received on accumulations is taxed.)

As Paid-up Insurance If:

1. You want some additional death benefits without cash outlay.
2. You are concerned that you might become uninsurable at a future date.
3. You want the greatest permanent estate value from your life insurance.
4. The policy is used for business partnership insurance and you need more permanent coverage each year as the value of the practice grows.

As Accumulations If:

1. You plan to use your life insurance equities as part of your retirement program.
2. You wish to build an emergency or loan fund.
3. You want to build an education fund independent of your insurance policies or other reserves.
4. You really do not need a reduction of your premium in that amount.

To Reduce Premium If:

1. You are on a tight insurance budget.
2. You are concerned only with the protection the policy gives.
3. These reductions in premium will help you afford to own additional coverages or investments.

For Annual Term Insurance If:

1. You want as much death benefit each year as possible, especially when you are young.
2. You wish to assure future purchases, should you lose your insurability.
3. The policy is used for business partnership purposes and you need substantially more temporary coverage each year as the practice grows.
4. You intend to borrow the cash value of your policy to pay your premiums, but want to keep the death protection at its highest level.*

* See Chapter 33, "Bank Funding–Minimum Deposit Plan—The Tax Gimmick."

24. *Loan Values*

When To Borrow On Your Life Insurance

"Doctor, if you ever need cash quickly and confidentially," your insurance agent pointed out, "you may borrow from my company, using this policy as collateral."

The time has come—you need cash. You own policies with ample cash values to satisfy your needs.

Should you borrow on your life insurance?

Before making a loan from any source, you should consider certain important aspects:

1. Interest rate charged
2. Ease of arranging loan
3. Time it takes to receive cash
4. Collateral necessary
5. Method of repayment
6. Expenses involved

Insurance loans generally cover these aspects favorably.

1. Most companies charge a fixed 5 per cent interest rate. National service (GI) policies call for 4 per cent. This is a pure interest rate that you pay only on the unpaid balance of the loan, not on the total amount you borrow. A loan of $1,000 from an insurance company as compared with one from the bank would show that:

If both interest rates were 5 per cent and both were paid back in monthly installments over 12 months, you would pay the bank $50 for the loan (5 per cent of $1,000), but would pay the insurance company only $25 (5 per cent of $500). With the insurance company, your unpaid balance declines from $1,000 to zero, thus averaging $500.

2. An insurance loan is easy to arrange. All you do is contact your agent for a standard loan form. He sends it to his company home office. The loan is granted without investigation, questions, or requirement of references. It is a confidential transaction.

3. Your insurance loan will reach you in four to ten days.

4. Your policy itself is your collateral. Varying with company rules, you can borrow up to 90 and sometimes 100 per cent of the cash value of your policy. This always guarantees the principal and interest to the company. If you die before the loan is repaid, the amount is simply deducted from your death benefits.

5. You can repay your loan at any time and in any amount over $5. As long as you pay the interest, as a matter of fact, you don't ever have to repay the loan. The amount, however, will be deducted at claim time. If you do not pay the interest, it will be added to your original loan. If your total debt exceeds the cash value of the policy, the latter is automatically cancelled.

6. Most insurance companies reserve the right to defer a loan from three to six months. However, this option is rarely exercised, and loans are quickly granted without charge of any kind.

At first glance, then, it may seem easiest and least costly to borrow on your insurance policy. However, there are important considerations that do not appear on the surface but are essential factors in making an intelligent decision.

Before you make that decision, consider these factors:

The amount you borrow from your insurance company is deducted, in the event of your death, from the proceeds of the policy. This may destroy the program you have built for the protection of your wife and children. You are actually borrowing, from your own estate, money which was originally intended for their protection.

Statistics strongly indicate that loans from life insurance policies are rarely repaid. In time, most of these debt-ridden policies are dropped, and the insurance intended for estate purposes is completely lost.

You must also remember that after you have received your loan and the value of the policy has decreased by the amount borrowed, the premiums remain the same that you paid for the full amount of protection. In a way, then, you are paying twice for your loan; once in the regular interest charge, and again for the protection that you are not receiving, since the loan is deducted from the proceeds upon your death.

Dividends from life insurance policies, which have been left to accumulate, are available to you at no interest charge and without the necessity of repayment to the company. They are, in effect, a savings account. After you have totalled the amount available from accumulated dividends on all your policies, you may find that you need to borrow much less than you had anticipated, or nothing at all.

Finally, remember that the interest rate in your insurance policy is fixed. You will always know exactly what the interest charges will be. If, at the time of your need, money is tight and interest rates are high, it may pay you to borrow from your insurance company. If, on the other hand, other sources make money available at a lower cost, you can utilize these sources and use your insurance policy as collateral to obtain a loan at lower cost. All financial institutions will gladly accept an assignment of cash values of a policy as collateral.

Look upon your policy, then, as an instrument of dual value when borrowing. It will either provide the actual cash or enable you to obtain the needed monies by serving as universally acceptable collateral.

25. *The Pension Power of Your Life Insurance*

The difference between an "old man" and an "elderly gentleman" is dependable income.

You can use many methods to provide yourself with reliable income when your earnings diminish or cease altogether due to old age.

One method is the use of life insurance and annuity policies as new sources of income.

All of your life insurance policies, except temporary term coverages, build equity in the form of guaranteed cash values. These, together with any dividends that may have accumulated over the years, represent a certain amount of cash available at retirement time. If you no longer need the death benefits provided by these policies, you may instruct the insurance company to pay this value to you in income instead of in a lump sum. Each company guarantees a certain amount of income for every thousand dollars of cash equity in your policy. The amount you will receive per month depends on how much value your policy has and how you want the income paid.

For example, if your life insurance policies contain a cash and dividend value of $100,000 at your age sixty, you may take one of the following:

1. Life Income without Refund

An income of $568 per month for as long as you live. When you die, the income ceases.

2. Life Income with Cash Refund

An income of $458 per month for as long as you live. If you die be-

TABLE 7 CHANCES OF LIVING FROM PRESENT AGE TO RETIREMENT AGE

Based on 1941 CSO Mortality Table

Present Age	*Retirement Age* *Per Cent* 55	60	65	70
20	79	71	61	48
21	79	71	61	48
22	80	72	61	48
23	80	72	61	48
24	80	72	61	48
25	80	72	62	48
26	81	72	62	49
27	81	73	62	49
28	81	73	62	49
29	81	73	62	49
30	82	73	63	49
31	82	74	63	49
32	82	74	63	50
33	82	74	63	50
34	83	74	63	50
35	83	75	64	50
36	84	75	64	50
37	84	75	64	51
38	84	76	65	51
39	85	76	65	51
40	85	77	65	51
41	86	77	66	52
42	86	78	66	52
43	87	78	67	52
44	88	79	67	53
45	88	79	68	53
46	89	80	68	54
47	90	81	69	54

TABLE 7 CHANCES OF LIVING FROM PRESENT AGE TO RETIREMENT AGE—Continued

Present Age	*Retirement Age* / *Per Cent* 55	60	65	70
48	91	82	70	55
49	92	83	70	55
50	93	84	71	56
51	94	85	72	57
52	95	86	73	58
53	97	87	74	58
54	98	88	75	59
55		90	77	60
56		92	78	61
57		93	80	63
58		95	81	64
59		98	83	65
60			85	67

fore you have received at least $100,000, the company pays the balance to your beneficiary.

3. Life Income with Ten Years Guaranteed

An income of $534 per month for as long as you live. If you die before you have received at least ten years of income, the company will continue payment to your beneficiary until the guaranteed ten years have been paid out. Thus, if you die at age sixty-two, two years after having received the first check, your beneficiary receives eight more years of payment.

4. Life Income with 15 or 20 Years Guaranteed

A life income of $595 and $450 per month, respectively, but with longer guaranteed periods.

5. Joint and Two-Thirds Survivor Income

You will receive $485 per month (assuming your wife is the same age as you) for as long as both of you live. After the first death, whoever survives will receive an income of two-thirds of that amount, or $323 for as long as he lives.

6. Joint and One-Half Survivor Income

The joint income provided is $585 per month until the first death, and one-half of that, or $292, for life to the survivor.

7. Joint and Full Survivor Income

An income of $471 per month is paid as long as you and/or your wife are alive. The death of one does not change the income to the survivor.

Actual amounts of monthly income vary with companies. Joint incomes are less if your wife is younger and more if she is older than you. Not all companies grant the joint income provision.

It does not matter what type of equity-building policies you own at retirement time, only how much cash and dividend values they contain. These values may have been accumulated through whole life or limited payment life plans, endowments, or retirement income plans. This enables you to use even low-cost life insurance policies, which you no longer need for family protection, to enhance your own retirement income.

It is easy to determine exactly how much you can expect from your policies at retirement. The key is the annuity factor which is found in all policies under a section entitled "Settlement Options" or "Modes of Optional Settlement." Under a heading of "Life Income" you will find how much the company will pay in monthly income for every $1,000 of cash available in the policy at any given age. Shown below are the annuity factors used by some of the major companies. Figures are based on a male, age sixty-five, and indicate how much life income (ten years guaranteed) each company will pay for every $1,000 of cash available. Figures relating to earlier or later retirement ages are relatively higher or lower.

Company *	*Factor*
Acacia Mutual	$6.45
Aetna Life	6.16
American National, Tex.	6.45
American United	6.06

* From the 1961 edition of *Flitcraft Compend*. Courtesy of Flitcraft Incorporated, New York, New York.

Company	*Factor*
Bankers of Iowa	6.16
Berkshire Life	6.24
Connecticut General	6.04
Connecticut Mutual	6.16
Continental Assurance	6.16
Equitable, N. Y.	5.90
Franklin Life	6.30
Guardian Life of America	6.16
John Hancock	6.04
Knights of Columbus	6.57
Lincoln National	6.11
Massachusetts Mutual	6.26
Metropolitan Life	6.16
Monarch Life	6.00
Mutual Benefit, N. J.	6.32
Mutual Life of New York	6.19
National Life, Vt.	6.04
Nationwide Insurance Co.	6.30
New England Life	6.21
New York Life	6.16
Northwestern Mutual	6.03
Occidental, Calif.	6.30
Pacific Mutual	6.16
Paul Revere	6.16
Penn Mutual	6.16
Phoenix Mutual	5.98
Prudential	6.04
Security Mutual, N. Y.	6.16
State Farm Life	5.92
Sun Life, Canada	6.02
Travelers	6.01
Union Central	6.20
Union Mutual	6.30
United States Life	6.30
Western & Southern	5.99

The most important aspects of life insurance for retirement are:

1. You cannot outlive your income. Your monies are actuarially so calculated as to last you a lifetime, no matter how long you live. This removes the fear of outliving your income.

2. You always know how much you will receive. This permits you to budget your living standard accordingly. Conversely, knowing the exact income you can expect, you are able to plan for additional income through investments or part-time work as your standard of living or the cost of living increases. Certainty of income is often more important than size.

3. You can protect your retirement monies against disability. Where other methods of accumulation must cease when your income is cut off by disability, your insurance contract will, by using the waiver of premium benefit, continue to operate and values will continue to increase as if you were still making regular contributions. This feature of self-completion is unique with life insurance. No other institution will make deposits into your retirement fund for you if you are unable to do so because you are disabled.

4. You create an immediate estate for your family if you die before retirement. Conversely, the more protection you purchase for the security of your loved ones, the more security you have provided for yourself.

5. Your monies are absolutely safe. Safety is a prime consideration when you establish a basic retirement plan. Although you may welcome a possible gain through more speculative ventures, you cannot afford the possible loss. A life insurance company spreads your premium dollars among thousands of investments, keeping in mind the importance of the safety of your funds. Stringent state regulations of investment practices by insurance companies and examinations to see that these are strictly adhered to afford you further protection.

6. You have no management problems. A life insurance policy automatically purchases perpetual expert management for you. You can devote your full energies to your practice and be certain that your monies are put to work for you under experienced management. Your equity always appreciates at a guaranteed pace and rate of interest. You have no problems of reinvestment, no decisions to make —decisions that must always be correct lest they take you off the course for which you set financial sail.

7. Your cash values are always available for emergencies or opportunities. You need not liquidate your plan to get your hands on quick, confidential, and guaranteed sums. On the other hand, you

can liquidate at the full guaranteed value shown in the policy even in a depression.

8. You can purchase the values of life insurance in convenient packages. You do not have to buy more or accept less than you want. Furthermore, you can budget payments in accordance with your individual needs.

9. You receive favorable tax treatment. The yearly growth of your cash value is not taxed as income. Most of the income you receive from life insurance at retirement is tax exempt. A small portion of that income is subject to tax but in the much lower bracket in which you will find yourself.

10. You are most likely to carry out your plan. There are many incentives for you to continue to save. Not only are you reminded by the company and agent but also, since your family security depends on your premium payment, you will continue to save money regularly and systematically. By the time your need for family protection is over, you will be well near the completion of your retirement plan.

It may surprise you to learn that one-seventh of all property wealth in the United States today consists of cash values on deposit with life insurance companies; cash values which will some day feed an elderly gentleman.

The same cash values also provide some five-hundred billions of dollars of insurance protection for American families, billions which in lump sum arc equal to five-sevenths of the total value of all tangible property in the United States.

Life insurance is a meaningful and important method of accumulating money for retirement income for men in all walks of life. A physician, whose time and energies must constantly be devoted to his profession, would be wise to use life insurance for his fundamental retirement method. Once he has established a comfortable guaranteed income, he can invest surplus monies in other more speculative, but less certain, ventures. At that point, he can enjoy a possible gain but can also afford a possible loss.

26. Policies Designed For Retirement

The Billion Dollar Gold Room of the San Diego Athletic Club should be of interest to every potential retiree. Ceilings and walls are completely papered with every conceivable type of security—a billion dollars of investments now serving as wallpaper. Among all this evidence of financial failure and shattered hopes, however, you will not find one life insurance policy!

Although you can accumulate the funds necessary for a guaranteed income with any policy other than term insurance, the retirement income policy has been designed to deliver the exact income desired at a preselected age. You can, for example, purchase a policy to yield a life income of $300 per month, starting at age sixty. You pay a premium which, with a conservative interest yield, will be adequate to create a reserve of dollars large enough at your age sixty to enable the company to pay you the stipulated life income.

The emphasis of the retirement income policy is on building up its cash value. There is also an element of protection. For each $10 per month income you purchase, you also receive $1,000 of coverage. A $300 per month retirement income policy will pay $30,000 to your family if you die prematurely. At one point, the cash value of your policy will exceed $30,000. The larger cash value then becomes the death benefit, and the insurance protection aspect ceases to exist.

These policies are made available to begin paying a life income starting with ages fifty-five, sixty, sixty-five, or seventy.

You may add the waiver of premium, disability income, and double indemnity for accidental death by paying an additional premium. The disability waiver of premium can be especially meaningful. During disability, the company would credit you with the premiums as if you were paying them. The cash value of your policy would continue to increase. If and when you recover, there would be no chargebacks for the increase in value which the company's premium credits has effected. If you remain disabled, your protection would continue to retirement age, at which point your income would begin.

Before you purchase a retirement income policy, consider these points:

1. Your death benefit is relatively small for the premium you pay. At age thirty-five, for example, a premium of $1,400 a year will give you a retirement income of approximately $390 per month starting at age sixty-five, and death protection of at least $30,000 until that time.

The same premium, however, will purchase $60,000 of whole life which will have enough cash value at age sixty-five to produce an income of approximately $330 per month for life. True, you end up with 15.5 per cent less income from the whole life policy but, if you have dependents, that is a small price to pay for 100 per cent more coverage from ages thirty-five to sixty-five.

2. Once you own a retirement income policy, it is not easy to change it back to a lower premium policy. To do that, you must be insurable. A coronary in your forties, while you still have dependent children, may cause you to wonder if the emphasis in your insurance program should not have been shifted toward more protection. Then, it is too late. Your company, knowing that your life span has been shortened, cannot agree to suddenly give an impaired risk more coverage for the same money or the same coverage for less money. On the other hand, either by contract guarantee or company practice, you can, for example, easily change a whole life policy to retirement income at a later date. The company will either get more money for the same death benefit, or the same money for less coverage.

3. If your primary objective is preparation for retirement and not necessarily protection, the retirement income policy will help you to attain that objective most efficiently.

4. You need new income when old income either diminishes or ceases. It is most unlikely that you will want to retire at age fifty-five, at the prime of your career. It is just as unlikely that your in-

come will not have been diminished considerably by the time you are seventy. The retirement income policy at age sixty-five may be the most practical. At that point, you may be ready or forced by circumstances to retire or at least to slow down. Yet this policy, as well as the others mentioned, have a built-in guarantee that permits you to choose an earlier retirement date. You will receive income in a smaller amount but at an earlier age. Thus, a $300 a month retirement income policy at age sixty-five, taken out at thirty-five, will provide approximately $212 per month at age fifty-five, $259 per month starting with age sixty, and so on.

This provision makes this policy more flexible and realistic than a retirement income policy at age fifty-five. The only way you can adjust that particular plan to a later retirement is to leave the money on deposit at interest for a few years and then draw income. Until age fifty-five, however, you will have had to pay a higher premium to maintain the policy and will have received relatively lower death protcction.

5. Many companies will permit you to use accumulated dividends to purchase additional life income. Since you want to realize the largest income possible, permit your dividends to accumulate at interest with the company and to increase your monthly checks at retirement.

6. Most retirement income policies are based on a life income, with at least ten years of payments guaranteed whether you live or not. If you want another method of payment, such as 15 or 20 years guaranteed, you will receive proportionately less income. Conversely, if you desire income only as long as you live with no guarantee period, you will receive a bit more income.

7. Sometimes, the total accumulated dividends are sufficient to enable you to request a joint and survivor income without reducing your own basic income. For example, the accumulated dividends on a $300 per month retirement income policy at sixty-five would yield enough additional income to enable the company to pay you $300 per month for as long as you live and continue half this income, or $150 per month, to your wife for as long as she lives.

Buy Retirement Income Policies If:

1. You are satisfied that your basic insurance program to protect your family is adequate.

2. You want to save money without management worries, with complete safety, and with as fair a yield as such safety warrants.

3. You want a tax-favored income you cannot outlive. The major portion of your retirement income will be tax-free since it is derived from your capital and thus considered a return of your own money. Only the portion attributable to gain above your original investment is taxable. At retirement, you will probably be in a lower bracket. This, together with old-age exemptions, will keep taxes extremely low.

4. You want a semicompulsory savings program which cannot be destroyed by disability.

5. You want high equities for a possible emergency or opportunity fund.

27. *How Annuities Can Serve You*

Someday, a majestic statue will be erected to honor the genius who developed the concept of an annuity.

Several major problems that have plagued the man about to retire have been:

1. In order to receive an adequate income which he cannot outlive, he must accumulate tremendous capital funds which must be depreciation-proof and which must earn a steady, predictable, and reasonable rate of interest.

2. It is difficult to accumulate large sums of money in days of high taxes, low investment yields, and rising costs.

3. One mistake, miscalculation, or "act of God" can shatter the most carefully devised retirement plan.

4. It is too difficult to accumulate enough capital to receive adequate income from interest. To draw on capital, in order to supplement interest income, only decreases the interest in turn. It is foolhardy to "eat off" capital since it may be gone before you are.

One excellent solution to these problems is the annuity, a contract which is devised to pay you an income for life. This income is actuarially calculated to tap both principal and interest in such proportion as to provide you with a fixed sum regularly, regardless of how long you live.

In an annuity contract, you receive a guaranteed minimum rate of interest. You also have the opportunity to add disability provisions which will complete the accumulation of funds for you during total disability. You accumulate your increasing cash values tax-free. When you receive your retirement income, it is only partially taxed.

Since part of each payment is a return of capital, only the portion that is interest is taxable as ordinary income. This amount is quite small. At age sixty-five, for example, an annuity income of

$2,200 per year is taxed on only $200. If you are then in the 30 per cent tax bracket, your tax is only $60. The same income from other sources would be considered fully as ordinary income and would be taxed for $660. If you qualify for retirement income credits under the Internal Revenue Code, the tax on the annuity income would be completely eliminated, and the amount payable on interest income would be reduced by a maximum of $240.

You must remember, however, that an annuity is a depleting asset. If estate preservation is important to you, you should not consider it.

An annuity is very similar to a retirement income policy except that it does not provide death protection other than a return of your money with interest, or the cash value if greater. For this reason, it is available even to men who are totally uninsurable. It also provides a bit more income than a retirement income policy since none of the premium is used for protection.

The income from an annuity can be arranged similarly to that of any life insurance policy; i.e., life income only, life income with guaranteed refund, life income with 10, 15, or 20 years guaranteed, and joint and survivor forms of income.

You can purchase an annuity in one of three ways:

Annual Premium Plan

You make your deposits each year until retirement and then receive your income. A doctor age thirty-fivc, for example, pays about $410 per year to age sixty-five and then receives an income of $100 per month for life, with at least ten years guaranteed.

Single Premium Deferred Annuity

You deposit one sum, leave it with the company at interest, and receive life income at a later date. A doctor age forty, for example, puts $15,000 into such an annuity. When he reaches age sixty-five, he receives approximately $145 per month for life, with refund of at least his original investment guaranteed even if he dies in the early stages of the "pay-off."

SINGLE PREMIUM IMMEDIATE ANNUITY

You deposit a lump sum and start receiving life income at once. A doctor age sixty-five, for example, pays $50,000 and immediately begins to receive $238 per month for life, with a guarantee of a return of the balance of his $50,000 investment, should he die before he has collected that much.

HOW CAN ANNUITIES BENEFIT YOU?

1. Suppose you, at age fifty, wish to assure yourself of $2,400 per year income starting with age sixty-five. If you can invest money at 4 per cent net after taxes and costs (which represents at least 6 per cent gross earnings throughout the accumulation and retirement periods), you would have to accumulate $60,000. This sum at 4 per cent net would produce $2,400 per year. An annuity can accomplish the same goal for $30,000. The difference of $30,000 can be used to increase your standard of living, to purchase an additional $2,400 per year annuity income, or to invest in more speculative ventures, since your necessary basic income is assured.

2. Suppose you, at age sixty-seven, are now retired and draw $4,800, or 4 per cent, per year from a capital investment of $120,000. You have no dependents and are not concerned about preserving the estate after your death. With an annuity, the same $120,000 can provide you with a life income of $9,750, or over 8 per cent, substantially tax-free. You have doubled your income, yet are assured that you will not outlive it. Even if estate conservation has some importance, you can still purchase almost $5,000 a year income with half of your capital and leave the rest at interest for eventual estate purposes.

3. You can guarantee a life income for aged parents, an invalid child, or a dependent relative through an annuity. Without management cares, you can be certain that your responsibilities toward these dependents are met whether or not you live. You can plan these annuities as gifts to qualify under favorable gift tax treatment.

4. If your estate will eventually go to charity, you can liquidate your holdings, use part of the money to purchase an annuity equal

to that income you would have been receiving had you not liquidated, and give the balance to charity now.

5. You can finance your son's extensive and expensive education in a speciality by replacing, with an annuity, some of the capital which is presently bringing you interest income. Since an annuity provides more income for less capital outlay, this move would release enough money to help with the education of your son.

6. An annuity can be an excellent depository for sudden windfalls or inheritances which you do not need but want to keep absolutely safe.

7. You can obtain an annuity without medical examination. With impaired health, you may wish to derive as much income as possible from your capital in order to compensate for the additional expenses incurred in preserving or improving your state of health. This is especially valid if estate preservation is of minor importance to you.

Your annuity, if underwritten by a mutual company, will also draw dividends. These can be taken in cash each year or left until retirement time to increase your life income.

All contracts, except for the single premium immediate annuity, have a loan value and a guaranteed interest charge of about 5 per cent. You can borrow quickly and confidentially at any time before retirement and repay the loan at your own convenience.

If you ever find it necessary to discontinue an annual premium annuity, the insurance company will either exchange it for a paid-up contract which will be for a lesser income but in ratio to your lesser investment, or you may liquidate it for cash. Until your annuity is approximately ten years old, you will take a loss when you cash it in. The earlier the liquidation, the greater the loss since it takes time for the absorption of initial expenses of issue. After the tenth year, however, you will receive your full investment plus interest.

If you are insurable, you can include, for a small additional premium, a provision in an annual premium annuity which obligates the company to make premium payments for you when you are totally disabled. Upon recovery, you do not have to pay any of these premiums back, nor are they deducted from your benefits.

If you must liquidate a single premium deferred annuity, you will receive the original purchase price plus interest. A small penalty is charged, however, if the cash-in occurs during the first three years. This compensates for the expenses involved in the issue of the annuity.

A single premium immediate annuity cannot be cashed in. Neither can any of the other annuities be liquidated, once the insurance company has commenced payments.

Be sure to supply evidence of your exact date of birth when you purchase an annuity. A photostat of your birth certificate is most advisable. Most companies require such proof before they will begin their payments. To avoid the danger of a loss of required evidence by fire, negligence, and the like, submit such documents with your original application.

Arguments against annuities and retirement plans are usually based on the fact that, producing a fixed income, they do not keep pace with the loss of the dollar's purchasing power.

It must be remembered, however, that during an inflationary period, your income also increases, enabling you to afford more investment in guaranteed annuities. The physician who reports that the $200 per month annuity he bought 30 years ago is no longer adequate for retirement, fails to recognize that his income may have tripled during these years, but he did not, however, increase his annuity accordingly.

Some physicians, having been skillful and fortunate and, therefore, successful in building large funds for retirement, utilize these sizable investments to guarantee the most important solution to their problem—adequate income they cannot outlive. Man, so far, has not been able to devise any other means to guarantee a substantial income which will not be exhausted before his death.

The death benefits of a retirement income policy and the disability benefits available with an annuity also can not be duplicated with any other type of investment. These benefits certainly are valuable to you.

Most economists will agree that retirement should be based on fixed guaranteed income supplemented with variable income, to compensate for the ups and downs of the economy. An annuity can provide that fixed guaranteed income to you at greatest advantage.

28. *The Variable Annuity*

THE RETIREMENT PLAN OF THE FUTURE—THE NEAR FUTURE?

"It will give you a fighting chance against inflation," is the way one insurance executive feels.

"It will destroy the public's hard-earned confidence in the insurance industry," predicts another.

"We will be able to compete against mutual funds," dreams the sales manager.

"It opens the door to federal regulation of the insurance industry," warns a company president.

The villain or hero in this emotion-packed argument is the variable annuity. Basically, this is a retirement plan that is intended to pay you an income based on the approximate purchasing power of the dollar rather than a fixed income, at your retirement. The premium you pay purchases a relative number of shares in the over-all investment program of the company.

Unlike a traditional life insurance company, this company invests its funds largely in diversified common stocks. On the theory that market prices of common stocks most often keep pace with the cost of living, proponents of the variable annuity expect your share in their over-all investment program to keep pace with economic fluctuations. When you are ready to retire, your income will be based on the total number of units, or shares, that you own and its relation to the earnings of the company each month.

You may receive more income one month and less the next. Theoretically, your higher income will absorb the declining purchasing power when there is inflation. During deflation, you will receive less but will also need less.

Since this concept is quite new as yet, and since less than a handful of companies have been authorized to issue such annuities, there is little actual experience on which either proponents or adversaries can base their judgments.

On the surface, it may seem that the variable annuity is just another name for a mutual fund. But the experience of life insurance is used not only to provide death protection if you die in the early stages of the program, but also to utilize the insurance annuity principle (the payment of a fixed income which expends both principal and interest over the period of a person's lifetime). This principle is the only scientific way known to man which guarantees that you cannot outlive your income. The difference between the variable and conventional annuities lies in the fact that the latter guarantees a fixed income for life, whereas the variable annuity guarantees a fixed proportion of the company's investment profits for life. Depending on these profits (or losses), the income varies.

The concept of a variable annuity has been the cause for intense verbal and legal warfare between economic factions in the United States. On one side of the battlefield stand the companies writing, or anxious to write, this form of annuity, joined by some established major insurance companies. On the other side are rallied other life insurance companies, securities dealers, and investment bankers.

The proponents of the concept of variable annuity argue that:

1. This form of annuity is essential in view of the continuing inflationary tendencies of our economy. A fixed income, they say, disregards the loss of purchasing power. Those who have retired in the last few years find the purchasing power of their annuity dollars reduced to half of what it was when the money was first deposited.

2. Since the market price of common stocks tends to keep pace with the cost of living, the variable annuity will provide a relatively stable income in terms of purchasing power at all times.

3. The progress made in medicine and the improved living conditions of the American people are reflected in a greater life expectancy. This increases the problem of providing realistic income for the many more who will live longer. The variable annuity provides that realistic income for life.

4. Few small investors have the funds, knowledge, energy, and time to devote to diversified investments. No one knows when he will die. Only through a variable annuity can the small investor enjoy the benefits of sound management of his money and obtain scientifically calculated income for life.

5. The variable annuity companies invest carefully. They do not buy stocks on margin and purchase only those stocks that are authorized by law for ownership by life insurance companies. Furthermore, they do not invest more than 1 per cent of their assets in any one company. They are also, for the protection of the public, under the strict supervision of the insurance department within the state in which they operate.

6. Variable annuity stock investments are also diversified through dollar cost averaging. These stocks are bought whether the market is up or down. They may reflect these ups and downs from time to time, but will keep pace with the gradual but steady rise in the long run.

7. While variable annuity units are accumulating, investment earnings are reinvested without charge. This increases the value of the units without the individual policyholder having to pay income taxes or brokerage fees on these increases. When annuity payments start, the policyholder enjoys a substantial tax exemption each year for life.

8. The policyholder can choose the type of annuity that best suits his needs, similar to a conventional annuity.

9. The policyholder enjoys many of the benefits of regular life insurance plans. Among these are: the right to name a beneficiary, to reinstate after ceasing premium payments, to borrow against or cash in, to discontinue the plan and continue his accumulated shares in the over-all investment portfolio of the company, and the privilege of a grace period for premium payment.

10. The policyholder should have a balanced program. Social security benefits and fixed income from life insurance policies, together with some income from variable annuities, are sufficient to serve as a basic income in the event of deflation, and the variable annuity will increase that basic income realistically during inflation.

Those opposed to the variable annuity object on the grounds that:

1. The life insurance industry has established an honorable record

of meeting its obligations in terms of promised fixed dollars. The public would lose confidence, they feel, if they could no longer depend on the exact promises of the industry.

2. The life insurance agent cannot serve two masters at one time. How can he be expected to sell the variable annuity when this sale depends on negating the value of the traditional and proven fixed-dollar concept?

3. Since insurance companies would be engaged in purchases of large amounts of common stocks, federal regulation and control might enter the picture.

4. Insurance companies, in search of large scale investments, would become direct threats to investment bankers who might lose the opportunity of underwriting future stock issues.

5. Mutual funds would suffer sharply since they cannot offer the public tax-free dividend accumulations and an income that the client cannot outlive.

6. The public may be enticed by promises of unguaranteed variable annuity benefits and may drop their existing life insurance policies.

7. The average family is alarmingly underinsured now. The variable annuity will drain off monies that should be used for additional family protection.

8. State and federal laws would have to be changed to permit proper control and regulation of this mixed business.

9. The cost of owning the variable annuity is too high. It hovers around 40 per cent of the first year's premium, 11 per cent of the next nine years' premiums, and 7 per cent thereafter.

10. Little is really guaranteed to the policyholder. During that period in which stocks go down but the cost of living remains high, the policyholder will suffer greatly. The fact that the market eventually rises does not compensate the retired man for his loss of bread and butter at the present time.

The prognosis seems to be that the variable annuity is here to stay. Until recently, only three commercial companies * have issued this plan. Their direct sales were limited to the states of Alabama, Arkansas, Kentucky, New Mexico, North Dakota, West Virginia,

* Variable Annuity Life Ins. Co., Washington, D.C. Equity Annuity Life Ins. Co., Washington, D.C. Participating Annuity Life Ins. Co., Fayetteville, Ark.

and the District of Columbia. The Prudential Insurance Company of America, outspoken proponent of this plan, won permission from the New Jersey legislature to sell variable annuities in that state. The law requires, however, that a purchaser must have a balanced share of fixed income sources before he may purchase a variable one. It seems only a matter of time before the other states will follow suit.

The Supreme Court of the United States also ruled that the sale of variable annuities will be under the control of both the Federal Securities and Exchange Commission and the insurance departments of the states.

No one can predict the eventual success or failure of this concept. History will judge whether it is truly a way of protecting yourself against inflation or whether it is a misdirected, pioneering effort resulting in immeasurable harm to the public.

29. *Is Your Life Insurance Policy an Investment?*

If you can guarantee that:

You will live to a ripe old age

You will never be disabled

You will invest money regularly

You will never make a poor investment decision

You will always enjoy a good income

Bonds will always yield a good stable return and will never be called

Stocks will always appreciate

Real estate will never require maintenance, repair, and management

Your investments will always have a ready market for liquidation

You will have extraordinary luck

Then you may not want to consider your life insurance policies as investments. As a matter of fact, based on these guarantees, your unqualified success as an investor is assured. Remove any of these guarantees, and your chances for success steadily diminish. Few men can afford failure.

Although your return on a life insurance policy may not appear spectacular, you do enjoy many benefits discussed in the previous chapters. This makes your policy a type of investment unlike any other.

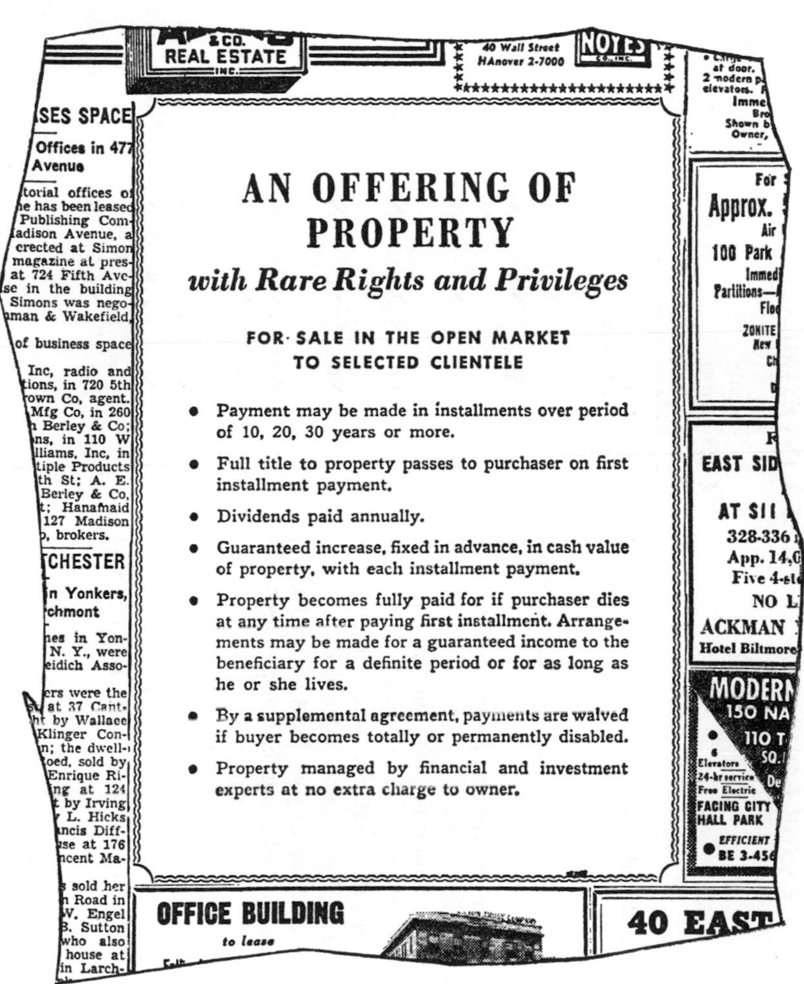

Courtesy of The Connecticut Mutual Life Insurance Company, Hartford, Connecticut.

TABLE 8 LIFE INSURANCE COMPARED TO OTHER INVESTMENTS

	Life Ins.	*Savings Acct.*	*Stocks*	*Corp. Bonds*	*U.S. Bonds*	*Real Est.*	*Mutual Funds*
1. Do you enjoy absolute safety of principal?	Yes	To $10,000	No	No	Yes	No	No
2. Can you liquidate your investment at any time to a guaranteed buyer at a contractual selling and purchase price?	Yes	Yes	No	No	Yes	No	No
3. Is it free from management, brokerage, and service fees chargeable directly to you?	Yes	Yes	No	No	Yes	No	No
4. Will it provide your family in lump sum all you had hoped to accumulate if you suddenly die?	Yes	No	No	No	No	No	No*
5. Are future investments made for you, without subsequent charge back, if you become disabled?	Yes	No	No	No	No	No	No
6. Can your investment pass to your heirs without going through costly estate administration and probate?	Yes	Yes†	Yes†	Yes†	Yes†	Yes†	Yes†
7. Does it enjoy special tax advantages?	Yes	No	No	No	No	No	No
8. Does it contain a guaranteed rate of interest on future loans?	Yes	No	No	No	No	No	No
9. Can you repay loans at your own convenience?	Yes	No	No	No	No	No	No
10. Is your investment guaranteed to appreciate in value each year?	Yes	No	No	No	Yes	No	No

* unless separate insurance is purchased
† if owned jointly with your wife or beneficiary

TABLE 8 LIFE INSURANCE COMPARED TO OTHER INVESTMENTS—Continued

	Life Ins.	*Savings Acct.*	*Stocks*	*Corp. Bonds*	*U.S. Bonds*	*Real Est.*	*Mutual Funds*
11. Are these increases free from income taxes?	Yes	No	No	No	No	No	No
12. Is it free from personal management and reinvestment worry?	Yes	Yes	No	No	Yes	No	Yes
13. Can it provide you or your heirs with a guaranteed life income?	Yes	No	No	No	No	No	No
14. Do you receive reminders to encourage systematic and regular investment?	Yes	No	No	No	No	No	No

30. The Medical Partnership

It was a beautiful funeral. Your widow, children, friends, and colleagues wept as the eulogy was given. Yes, you certainly were loved and respected. This, in itself, is a partial reward for your many years of devotion to your profession and community.

Your family will be able to get along comfortably. It takes money to send the boys through college. Your partner will take care of that. Both of you worked hard to build the practice to the heights it reached before your accident. Your life had not been a useless one.

Two weeks later, a moving van pulled into your widow's driveway. Husky workers unloaded a desk, a chair, three examining tables, several cartons of books, a dictating machine, your instrument cabinets, a large box of medical instruments, a carpet, one electric typewriter, and two Van Gogh reproductions. Your partner had fulfilled his legal obligation and returned one-half of the physical assets of your practice to your widow.

As existing accounts receivable are collected, your partner will send one-half of them to your family. Of course, he will deduct your share of any expenses incurred while you were still together.

So, after years of devotion to a practice that afforded you an excellent income, your legacy consists of some furniture and a small income to your family for a limited period of time.

Your widow is shocked at the realization that the fine income you brought home was based on intangibles that were interred with your bones—your ability, training, skill, and reputation.

In the absence of any provision to the contrary, your partner is obligated only to turn over one-half of the depreciated tangible assets of the partnership, plus one-half of the accounts receivable, after expenses, that accrued while you were alive. Obviously, such an arrangement is utterly immoral and unfair. Your interest in the partnership certainly exceeds the values described.

A buy and sell agreement between partners is the most equitable solution to this problem. It provides that:

1. The surviving partner will purchase the interest of the deceased for a stipulated price and obtain full ownership of the practice.

2. The estate of the deceased partner will sell its interest at the predetermined price and will relinquish any further rights to the practice. With this arrangement, the survivor acquires sole ownership of the practice while the family of the deceased receives a fair price for its interest.

An equitable solution has been found; yet, it requires immediate cash to be carried out.

A life insurance policy is normally used to provide the funds necessary to make the agreement practical.

Let us examine a hypothetical case. Doctors Ashley and Benson, equal partners, value their practice at about $100,000. A buy and sell agreement is drawn wherein the buy-out price is stipulated to be $50,000. Dr. Ashley purchases a $50,000 policy on the life of Dr. Benson, who purchases the same on the life of Dr. Ashley. Subsequently, Dr. Ashley dies. Dr. Benson receives the $50,000. He turns this money over to widow Ashley in return for properly documented release of all interest in the partnership.

This example is, of course, an oversimplification, but the solution is applicable in most cases. Possible complications and alternate methods of arranging a buy-out should be considered. For example:

1. It may be wise to appoint a corporate trustee, such as a bank, to handle the buy-out. A corporate trustee is perpetual, impartial, and can be depended on to execute the agreement with speed and precision.

2. Provision may have to be made to re-evaluate the worth of the practice periodically. If the insurance monies fall short of a fair evaluation, additional coverage may have to be purchased or a formula may have to be devised to pay the difference.

3. In a practice of more than two partners, it may be simpler for the partnership to purchase and own policies on each member rather than to apply the "criss-cross" method. This may, however, create

other problems; for example, since these policies are partnership assets, they are subject to the claims of creditors.

4. Since your whole estate picture will be influenced by your buy and sell agreement, it is important to determine the answers to the following questions as they apply to your own circumstances:

a. Who should own and pay for the policies?
b. Who should be the beneficiary?
c. What are the tax implications to the surviving partner and the widow?
d. How should the buy-out be arranged for the most advantageous tax treatment?
e. How should the practice be evaluated and re-evaluated?
f. How shall the surviving partner buy back the policy on his life? It contains cash equity and is now owned by the estate of the deceased partner.

Your C.P.A., who is familiar with your own particular situation, should most definitely be consulted. The tax laws and implications relating to professional partnerships and buy-outs are complicated.

5. Only an attorney experienced in this field should prepare the legal documents designed to accomplish a buy-out. There are sample agreements available from various sources, but they should not be used to save attorneys' fees. The agreement must be tailor-made to your needs in order to be effective and dependable. It must also blend in with your over-all estate plan.

6. After your accountant has checked out those factors pertaining to tax and business implications, you should call your insurance advisor to coordinate the necessary policies with the general design of the buy and sell agreement.

Many types of policies can be purchased to fund a buy and sell agreement. They are:

TERM INSURANCE

If the partners have limited funds and are interested solely in the death protection of insurance, 5-, 10-, or 20-year term coverage can provide it.

Whole Life Insurance

The use of permanent, equity-building coverage will also establish a reserve fund for emergencies, quick and confidential business loans at a guaranteed rate of interest, excellent collateral and, as the equity grows, an increasingly valuable partnership asset. In later years, the cash value of the insurance can provide the funds for retirement buy-out of a partner.

Retirement Income Insurance

High equity policies can be used if ample premium monies are available and if the partners wish to prepare larger funds for a buy-out at retirement.

In most instances, whole life insurance is the most advantageous since it is the least expensive of all equity-building policies and is flexible enough to adjust to most situations.

Whether or not you outlive your partner, a buy and sell agreement funded by life insurance is to your advantage. If you die first, your family will receive a fair price for your interest in the practice; if your partner dies first, you will receive immediate funds with which to purchase the practice.

Whether you live to retirement or not, a funded buy and sell agreement is to your advantage. If you reach retirement age, the insurance which has been the financial foundation of the agreement during your productive years will become a basic retirement program for the rest of your life. If you do not live to retirement, the insurance affords financial security to your family.

A buy and sell agreement funded by life insurance is a must for the medical partnership.

31. *Charitable Bequests*

" 'Tis Often Better To Give . . ."

Medical school closed due to lack of funds. Apply at nearest state medical school.

This sign may greet your son when he arrives at the door to your alma mater.

Medical schools, other colleges and universities, medical research centers, churches, hospitals, civic and fraternal organizations, and countless other worthy groups are in desperate need of funds. Their investments are yielding less income, their operating and expansion costs are steadily increasing, and the influx of large donations is diminishing due to excessive taxation of the prospective donor.

Many physicians have close sentimental ties to their medical schools and fraternities. They would like to make substantial and meaningful gifts. High income taxes and rising living costs, however, prevent such large gifts. They cannot provide bequests through their estates since they do not have enough left to support both family and charity after their estates have shrunk because of taxes and administration costs.

One excellent way to make a gift or bequest to a school or any other charitable organization is through life insurance. Its many advantages make it almost comparable to a delicious cake with an even more attractive icing.

THE CAKE

1. You can make your contribution with relatively small annual outlays from income.

2. Your estate, after death, is not diminished nor is your family deprived of any portion of it.

3. Your bequest is not subject to estate taxes, fees, administrative costs, or the like, but is paid to your designated school or charity immediately, in cash and in full.

4. If you become disabled, you can arrange for your contributions to be continued by the insurance company. Upon your death, the school receives the full benefit as if you had continued the premium contributions yourself.

5. The cash and loan features of your gift policy can be used by your favorite institution for emergency purposes while you are still alive.

6. You can avoid all publicity, if you so desire, since the gift is made directly through the insurance company to your designated charity. On the other hand, you may make the gift as a living memorial to yourself or someone else.

7. You can bequeath enough to make it meaningful to the recipients, yet can contribute annually through budgeted premium payments without affecting your over-all standard of living.

8. Your gift will not throw management burdens (such as would the sale or rental of property) on the recipient.

9. You can make insurance gifts confidentially, simply, and without legal assistance.

THE ICING

1. You can contribute up to 20 per cent of your adjusted gross income and take a deduction on your federal income tax. You can donate up to 30 per cent if the recipient is a church, tax-exempt educational institution, or tax-exempt hospital, and take the full deduction.

2. You do not have to pay federal gift tax on these contributions.

3. Your gift is not considered part of your estate for federal estate tax purposes.

This triple tax advantage is available to you if you purchase a life insurance policy and make the school or charity absolute owner and beneficiary. The death benefit goes untaxed to the designated charity. The value of your gift is much greater through life insurance proceeds than it would be as small, annual contributions to the charity.

Depending on your income tax bracket, every premium is partially supported by the federal government in the percentage you would normally have to pay in taxes. If you are forty years old, the actual cost of an annual gift to charity, using life insurance, can be illustrated as follows:

Amount of Insurance	*Annual Premium*	*Actual Cost in Various Tax Brackets* 34%	43%	50%	62%
$10,000	$300	$198	$171	$150	$114
25,000	750	495	428	375	285

If you have a policy which you no longer need, you may assign it to the favored organization. Its cash value will be considered a tax-free gift, the future premiums will be tax-deductible, and the death proceeds will escape estate taxes.

There are other ways you can use life insurance policies to enjoy some of the tax advantages discussed. You may, for example:

1. Take out life insurance with many insurance companies, for personal use, but assign all dividends to your school. No gift taxes need be paid, but the premium is not deductible.

2. Assign only a portion of your dividends. For example, if you purchase a $25,000 policy, you may make a gift of the dividends on $5,000 of it. The same tax rules apply.

3. Name your school as a secondary beneficiary to receive all monies if your beneficiary predeceases you. Although you cannot deduct the premiums paid, monies paid at death pass to the school without gift or estate taxes.

4. Stipulate, in arranging your policies on income provisions, that any income still due your beneficiary at her death be continued to your school.

Intricate bequest arrangements can be made through the use of trusts and annuities for which you pay in one lump sum. A life insurance advisor can take you by the financial hand and guide you through the labyrinth of useful bequest ideas. Your attorney can legally formalize them.

More and more state medical schools are being established. In many instances, these tax-supported institutions tend to offer better facilities and higher salaries to their staffs. Private schools find themselves forced to accept governmental funds to subsidize building and research programs. There are usually strings attached to these funds. Lack of money makes it difficult to hire and hold top-notch personnel. To help this problem to an acceptable solution, the National Fund for Medical Education, in New York, administers gifts and bequests from doctors, businessmen, and other philanthropists. Upon your request, they will endow a specific school with your funds.

Life insurance is certainly one of the most advantageous tools available to purchase immortality for yourself, a sound economy for your school, an opportunity for your children, and the continued independence of our free society.

All this and a tax break, too.

32. The Tax-Sheltered Annuity

Working for a nonprofit organization can be most profitable.

Full- or part-time employees of nonprofit hospitals, medical schools, health agencies, research foundations, and other tax-exempt institutions can take advantage of some favorable tax breaks.

Under the Technical Amendments Act of 1958, these institutions are permitted to purchase tax-sheltered annuities for you.

Provided the money is put into an annuity, an amount of up to 20 per cent of your current compensation can be set aside by your employer for that purpose without your having to pay current federal income tax on it. (Check, however, to determine if the premium paid for an annuity is considered current income if your state has a state income tax.) For example, if you are a full-time employee of a qualifying institution, with a salary of $10,000 a year, you can instruct the employer-organization to pay you only $8,000 a year and to use the other $2,000 toward the purchase of an annuity. You do not pay income tax on the $2,000 withheld. You may also arrange for future salary increases to be made in the form of premiums toward this annuity.

If you are not currently employed by a qualifying organization, but contemplate such a move, you may negotiate the purchase of a tax-sheltered annuity as one condition of employment.

If you have already served for several years with a qualifying organization, you can benefit further by the use of an exclusion allowance. Suppose your salary has been $10,000 a year for the last four years, and the hospital or other qualified employer has never paid any premiums toward an annuity for you. Your employer's allowance for premiums this year would be 20 per cent of your compensation, or $2,000, times the number of years you have been employed, a whopping $8,000 tax-exempt to you. If the institution has previously paid something toward an annuity and you have excluded the amount from your taxable income, your exclusion allowance would be 20 per cent of your current salary times the number of years employed, less all excluded premiums previously paid. To illustrate, if your salary has been $10,000 for eight years and the organization has paid $8,000 toward an annuity or pension plan, your current allowance would be $2,000 for eight years, or $16,000, minus the $8,000 already paid, or $8,000.

As a part-time employee, you must add up your time of service until it is the equivalent of a year's full-time work. If you have worked quarter-time for four years, for example, count your time of service as one full year. The same applies to the computation of current compensation. For purposes of exclusion allowances, monies you have received over a period equivalent to one full year of service represent current compensation, even though they may have been paid to you over a four-year-period. Let us say that you have received $4,000 a year for quarter-time employment over the last six years. This represents one and one-half years of full-time service at $16,000 per year. Your exclusion allowance would be 20 per cent of $16,000, or $3,200, multiplied by the years of service which are considered as one and one-half, or a total of $4,800. This sum can be paid by the employer toward an annuity without your having to pay income tax on it. Four years later, you would again have the equivalent of a full year's service with an exclusion allowance of another $3,200.

Only when you receive annuity benefits upon retirement, do you pay taxes. Considering that you will be in a much lower tax bracket, that annuities receive very favorable tax treatment, and that you will be entitled to old-age exemptions and larger medical deductions, you may have to pay little or no taxes at all on your annuity income.

You may designate your wife as joint-annuitant without paying a gift tax. Furthermore, in the event of your death, the value of any future payments to be made to her will not be subject to estate tax.

This form of a tax-sheltered annuity may well be a good incentive for you to investigate the possibility of part-time employment with a tax-exempt institution. Unless congressional legislation is passed permitting the physician to set up advantageous deferred-compensation plans, it may be the only means for you to provide for your retirement with dollars that have not yet been ground through the income tax mill.

33. *Bank Funding—Minimum Deposit Plan*

The Tax Gimmick

No longer must you build a better mousetrap to have the world beat a path to your door. You can accomplish the same result by coming up with anything that has a tax "angle" to it.

The key to the latest tax angle in life insurance is the deductibility of interest payments. If you borrow money to pay a premium, the interest you must pay for that money is tax-deductible. If you are in a high enough tax bracket, this can mean substantial savings for you.

If a loan is obtained from a bank, it is called "bank funding." If the premium monies are borrowed directly from the insurance company, this concept is most often referred to as "minimum deposit."

Here is how the idea is put into operation:

You obtain a large policy, for example, $100,000, from a company which has a special plan for this purpose. At your age forty, the premium would amount to approximately $2,860 a year. This special policy has a cash value in the first year of $2,000. You may borrow 95 per cent of that amount during the first year, or $1,900. Therefore, after making out the loan form, you must come up with only $960, and the premium is considered paid. The company charges you 5 per cent on the money you have borrowed. This, amounting to $95, is tax deductible.

In the second year, your premium is still $2,860. But you now have a dividend credit of $268. Deducting this amount, the net premium due the company is $2,592. Your cash value, meanwhile, has increased by $2,100. You may borrow 95 per cent of that, or $1,995, come up with the difference between the loan and the net premium, or $597, and your second year is paid. Now you are charged with interest on both years, $195, and that charge is tax deductible.

This procedure is followed each year.

The yearly dividends are expected to increase, thus lowering the net premium you must pay. The yearly increase in cash value is large enough to almost absorb the premium due that year. The amount of your loan gets larger as does the interest charge. The more interest you pay, the more you can deduct. The greater your deduction, the lower the over-all cost of your insurance.

The facts are more clearly illustrated in Table 9, page 142.

The actual cost over a 20-year-period, based on your being in the 50 per cent bracket, is lower than any form of term insurance you can buy. You should be aware of the fact that in the event of your death, the amount of the loan will be deducted from the $100,000. Yet, the decrease in death protection is much more gradual than that with decreasing term insurance. Many companies will, for an additional nominal premium, even cover you for the amount of the loan so that when you die this extra protection can pay off the loan and your full $100,000 can remain intact for your family. Others will use your dividends to purchase enough term coverage to pay off the loan at your death. This, of course, is in lieu of using them to reduce premiums.

You can add disability waiver of premium to this plan, obligating the company to pay your $2,860 a year premium while you are permanently disabled. While you are disabled, you can go right on borrowing the increase in cash value, if you so desire, but use these funds to supplement your income. On the other hand, you can then stop borrowing and permit the increase in cash value to start repaying your loan, which in turn automatically increases your death benefit.

This plan also has the advantage of permitting you to use investment hindsight. If you normally invest in more speculative ventures, you may find the investment picture in a certain year to be poor. You can then put your investment funds into the cash value of this policy where you will be guaranteed a conservative rate of interest,

TABLE 9 MINIMUM DEPOSIT PLAN—MALE, AGE 40

Policy Years	*Premium Less Div.*	*Cash Value End of Yr.*	*Year's Increase in Cash Value*	*Amount You Can Borrow*	*Total Loan on Which You Pay Interest*	*Interest 5 Per Cent on Total Loan*	*Difference You Pay*	*Total You Pay Before Tax Credit*	*Actual Cost to You If in 50 Per Cent Bracket*	*Death Benefit Less Total Loan*
1	$2,860	$ 2,000		$1,900	$ 1,900		$960	$ 960	$960	$98,100
2	2,592	4,100	$2,100	1,995	3,895	$ 95	597	692	644	96,105
3	2,540	6,100	2,000	1,900	5,795	195	640	835	737	94,205
4	2,487	8,100	2,000	1,900	7,695	290	587	877	732	92,305
5	2,433	10,200	2,100	1,995	9,690	385	438	823	630	90,310
6	2,377	12,200	2,000	1,900	11,590	485	477	962	719	88,410
7	2,332	14,300	2,100	1,995	13,585	580	337	917	627	86,415
8	2,286	16,400	2,100	1,995	15,580	679	291	970	630	84,420
9	2,239	18,500	2,100	1,995	17,575	779	244	1,023	633	82,425
10	2,194	20,600	2,100	1,995	19,570	879	199	1,078	638	80,430
11	2,149	22,700	2,100	1,995	21,565	979	154	1,133	643	78,435
12	2,104	24,800	2,100	1,995	23,560	1,078	109	1,187	648	76,440
13	2,059	26,900	2,100	1,995	25,555	1,178	64	1,242	653	74,445
14	2,014	29,000	2,100	1,995	27,550	1,278	19	1,297	658	72,450
15	1,969	31,100	2,100	1,969	29,519	1,378		1,378	689	70,481
16	1,926	33,200	2,100	1,926	31,445	1,476		1,476	738	68,555
17	1,884	35,300	2,100	1,884	33,329	1,572		1,572	786	66,671
18	1,842	37,400	2,100	1,842	35,171	1,666		1,666	833	64,829
19	1,802	39,500	2,100	1,802	36,973	1,759		1,759	879	63,027
20	1,762	41,500	2,000	1,762	38,735	1,849		1,849	924	61,265

20-Year Summary of average yearly cost to you after tax credit: 0% = $1,087 30% = $779 40% = $676 50% = $574 75% = $317

usually about 2.5 per cent tax free. When the outside picture improves, you can borrow this money and not leave it idle at any time.

When you reach retirement age, you can repay your loan at one time, with monies earned in outside investments, and take advantage of the guaranteed life income options that all life insurance policies contain.* At that time, it might be your most advantageous method of obtaining an income you cannot outlive.

There are three basic dangers to this type of policy:

1. At some future date, the advantage of tax-deductibility may be disallowed by congressional legislation. The Internal Revenue Code of 1954 disallowed future tax deduction of interest paid on loans designed for the purchase of single premium annuities (annuities paid for in one lump sum). This was permitted under prior codes.

2. Your tax bracket may decrease. What was advantageous to you while you were in a 50 per cent bracket, may be most burdensome to you should you be taxed in a lower bracket. With a decreased income, you would lose the benefit of high deductions and yet would be forced to pay the same amount of money.

3. The company might lower its dividends, which would change your required net premium.

Don't consider minimum deposit or bank loan plans unless:

You are in at least the 40 per cent bracket.

You need additional coverage.

You do not wish to divert investment capital toward equity building insurance.

You keep your financial records in perfect order at all times (these interest deductions may invite closer scrutiny of your tax return).

You are willing to take the risk that interest may be disallowed or that your tax bracket may change. Neither of these events, by the way, spells doom. Yet, they do remove the original advantage of this type of program.

A note of caution:

Beware of the agent who urges you to drop or discontinue premium payment on existing permanent policies in order that you may take out minimum deposit. In few instances does this represent an advantage to you. (You can minimum pay your present policies, if

* See Chapter 25, "The Pension Power of Your Life Insurance."

such is necessary.) This practice was one of the main reasons that the New York Insurance Department recently placed tight restrictions on the solicitation of this coverage by companies and agents within its jurisdiction. Company officials are also concerned about the temptation to upset existing plans and are closely supervising their sales forces to prevent such action.

34. *Estate Planning*

Put Order Into Your Estate

When you die physically, your financial life will continue for a maximum of 15 months. This is the length of time allowed by law for payment of your federal estate taxes.

How much will your estate have to pay?

What funds will be available to pay these costs?

How much of your estate will remain to benefit your dependents in accordance with your desires?

Can you, in some way, minimize these taxes?

How about those executor's, accountant's, appraiser's fees, court costs, and other expenses?

What will these costs be?

How will they be paid?

Will your objective for the well-being of your loved ones materialize?

Only through competent estate planning can these and related matters be determined.

Estate planning, in a general sense, is over-all financial planning to benefit you during your lifetime and your loved ones after your death. It deals with the accumulation, distribution, and administration of all forms of property. This consists of insurance, annuities, stocks, bonds, mutual funds, land, realty, bank accounts, equipment, jewelry, business or professional interests, and anything else of value. You spend a lifetime creating and accumulating these assets. Without proper planning, the distribution of them may unnecessarily fall short of your original goal: your well-being during your life and the security of your family after your death.

In 1955, a New York millionaire was accidentally killed. His estate, amounting to over twelve million dollars, was not properly planned. By the time all debts and inheritance taxes were paid, the estate had shrunk to three million dollars, or 25 per cent. Six million dollars were paid to the federal government while over a million dollars were paid to the state of New York. Financial and legal experts are convinced that these amounts could have been drastically reduced through planning.

The death of the wife of a well-known American crooner forced him to liquidate, at a loss, stocks, two mansions, and even a stable of race horses in order to meet an inheritance tax of one million dollars due in cash. Estate planning could have eliminated, or at least lessened, the financial blow.

Few physicians are qualified to plan their own estates. Although volumes of technical books have been written on the subject, few individuals anywhere can undertake an over-all estate plan. It requires the services of a team: an attorney, insurance advisor, trust officer, and accountant. Each can contribute his specialized knowledge. Since any estate planning requires legal documents, your attorney becomes your key man. Only he can put a plan into action; however, it is the insurance agent who often calls the need for estate planning to your attention. His fundamental knowledge and training are broad enough to enable him to recognize the existing problem, yet he cannot give legal advice. The attorney, on the other hand, can execute the legal documents; yet, by his code of ethics, he cannot solicit this type of work.

Therefore, you must initiate action. Here are some of the ways you can begin:

1. On paper, list your short- and long-range objectives. These could include such items as:

Creating an educational fund for your children.

Providing immediate death benefits for burial.

Disposing of personal items, such as a stamp collection, to a particular son.

Providing a home for your family.

Guarantying an income to your family until the children are of age, and to your wife for the rest of her life.

Accumulating an emergency fund.

Establishing income for your wife which cannot be dissipated through incompetence or outside influences.

Providing for financial management of your estate.

Limiting or broadening control of assets going to children.

Containing or widening the influence your wife may have on the children's wealth.

Your investment and retirement plans for old age.

Financial considerations for other dependents, such as parents or invalid brothers.

Bequests to institutions.

Add any other matters relating to short- or long-range planning.

2. Next, list all your assets, including bank accounts, real estate, mortgages, securities, accounts receivable, personal and jointly owned property, life insurance.

3. From these assets, deduct any loans, notes, and accounts payable.

4. Jot down your total net assets.

Looking over your short- and long-term objectives, ask yourself three questions.

1. Do I have the legal papers which direct the disposition of my assets in accordance with these stated objectives?

2. Do I have assets adequate to fund all my objectives after estate and administration costs?

3. What will these estate taxes and administration costs be?

If the answer to the first question is in the negative, your estate planning should begin with your attorney. Call him and outline your desires and he will draw the documents needed to achieve them. If the answer to the second question is in the negative, call your insurance advisor. He will recommend ways of creating an immediate increase in your estate value through insurance. If you do not know the answer to the third question, contact your accountant and he will give you a general idea as to what will remain in your estate after the obligatory tax and administrative costs have been met.

Your initial approach will cause your advisors to recognize your interest and help you develop it further until an estate plan is established. Encourage your accountant and attorney to keep you informed of any new or existing legislation that may affect you. Make it clear to them that you seek new ideas. This will enable them to contact you with information without violating their codes of ethics.

Most major insurance companies make excellent estate-planning literature and forms available to their agents. Have your agent supply you with some of these pamphlets and ask him to prepare a confidential survey form for you, for which service, by the way, there is no charge. Authorize him to contact your accountant and attorney with this information. Among the three of them, they will undoubtedly come up with some suggestions of value to you. This method is usually the most convenient, economical, and productive.

Each of your advisors will utilize the tools of his trade as a contribution to your over-all estate plan. You should be familiar with the tools and how they can apply to your well-being. Although the following descriptions are oversimplifications, they are intended as a quick excursion into the areas of thought your advisors will investigate.

THE WILL

Since it represents the heart of any estate plan, a will may be the first tool to be utilized. A will is a legal document which directs the distribution of your property at death. It should be reviewed periodically in light of changing personal conditions. An attorney is best qualified and legally authorized to draw a will.

THE BUY AND SELL AGREEMENT

Most medical partnerships operate with a buy and sell agreement. It is a contract that provides for the estate of a deceased physician to receive the fair value of his interest in lump sum and/or income for a number of years. It further provides for the surviving partner, or partners, to acquire full ownership of the practice. It may also regulate the share of accounts receivable a disabled physician may receive and the length of time this full or gradually decreasing share must be paid to him. Although it usually contains other additional provisions, these are the most important for estate planning purposes.

Most buy and sell agreements are funded in part or in whole by life insurance. What other instrument can provide the immediate monies necessary for quick execution of such an agreement?

As one of the partners reaches retirement age, life insurance equities can be used to provide him with a life income in return for his equity in the practice. If one of the partners suddenly dies, the insurance money can be used to compensate the widow adequately for his interest without throwing the practice into financial chaos. Cash values of life insurance, used for funding, enhance the value of the partnership during life.

Insurance

Insurance is a most convenient way to create an immediate estate, to build a foundation for retirement with favored tax treatment, to obtain tax-free income when you are disabled, and to conserve your assets when catastrophic medical expenses arise.

Life insurance policies can serve to pay estate and other taxes upon your death, thus making it unnecessary for your estate to liquidate valuable properties under adverse conditions.

Other policies, such as endowment, retirement income plans, and annuities, can represent a guaranteed life income to you and your wife with favorable tax treatment.

Insurance can also be used in arranging a life insurance trust, wherein a trust company manages the money derived from insurance. Through a trust arrangement, you can often effect considerable income and estate tax savings.

Properly arranged ownership and control of life insurance policies can often reduce your gross taxable estate, thus saving large sums without endangering the original purposes of the policies.*

With intelligent application, life insurance can be used to fund most estate objectives.

Disability income policies can provide you with a tax-free income which not only replaces your earnings, but also makes it unnecessary to tap your reserves which have already gone through the tax mill.

Major medical insurance can absorb your larger medical expenses, thus again preserving hard earned assets.

* See Chapter 14, "Should Your Wife Own Your Life Insurance?"

THE MARITAL DEDUCTION

The marital deduction is a special deduction granted to the estate of a married person. Under certain conditions, you may leave your wife up to 50 per cent of your adjusted gross estate (gross estate less funeral and administration expenses, claims against the estate and other items) and have this percentage exempt from federal estate tax.

Although the advantages of the marital deduction can decrease your estate tax liability tremendously, it will increase your wife's estate accordingly. Thus, the marital deduction may only postpone payment of federal estate taxes.

The marital deduction is a tricky matter. The Revenue Code sets up definite conditions under which your assets can be considered for the deduction. Your attorney and your accountant should most certainly be consulted to determine if the arrangement for the distribution of your assets will qualify.

GIFTS

Gifts can have important implications on income and estate taxes. Basically, you may give away $30,000 over your lifetime in property or cash without having to pay gift taxes. If your wife joins you in the gift, this sum becomes $60,000. In addition to this total you may give in a lifetime, you can give up to $3,000 per year (or $6,000 if your wife participates) to any number of persons without paying gift taxes. The person to whom you make the gift is also exempt from paying taxes.

You can accomplish the following tax savings through gifts:

1. The gift is removed from your estate and eventually winds up in the estate of another, who presumably will be in a lower tax bracket.

2. Even if the abovementioned tax-free allowances are exceeded, you still save on the lower gift tax as compared to the estate tax. (Although gift taxes were devised to prevent you from giving your assets away while you are still alive, thereby escaping estate taxes, the gift tax is usually lower than the estate tax.)

3. If you gift property to an especially constructed, qualified trust, the income from it is removed from your high income tax bracket to someone's lower bracket. This saves you income taxes and may actually make it profitable for you to give away taxable income from property or investments.

Gifts can be made to children, trusts, charitable institutions, colleges, and a variety of other recipients.

Remember, however, that a gift cannot be taken back. The indiscriminate use of gifts can be disastrous and leave you without needed income or assets at a critical moment.

Special note must be taken of the "contemplation of death" regulation in making gifts. If you should die within three years of the time you made your gift, it may still be included in your estate for tax purposes. The government considers such a gift made "in contemplation of death." Therefore, if any gifts are recommended, make them as early in life as possible.

Again, the Revenue Code relating to gifts is very complicated. Professional advice is essential.

Trusts

A trust, generally, is a written agreement wherein a person or corporation holds legal title to property and manages it for someone else, under specific terms.

You can create a trust through your will. Known as a testamentary trust, its provisions become effective upon your death.

You can also create a living trust, with provisions effective while you are alive.

You can set up a life insurance trust. The death proceeds of your policies would be paid to a trustee who would manage them in accordance with the terms of a trust agreement.

There are numerous subdivisions of these basic trusts, depending on who retains control, who pays premiums, what rights are reserved to the trustee, and countless other considerations.

Trusts are usually created for specific purposes. These might be:

1. To assure yourself of sound and experienced management of your properties after your death.

2. To relieve yourself of management worries while you are alive

so that you can devote full time and a clear mind to your own profession.

3. To protect a member of the family, such as an aged parent or ill child, who does not have the physical or mental capacity for management.

4. To save taxes.

To accomplish these and many other purposes, the trustee supervises the management and investment of the property involved, and sees to it that the accomplishments of his work coincide with your original goal. He is compensated for his efforts by various formulae, depending on the value of the trust, the income derived from it, the principal involved, and other legal and economic factors prevailing in the state of your residence.

A bank often serves as trustee; it has characteristics most important to the fulfillment of your goals. Besides having continuous existence, it also exercises impartiality, has excellent sources of information, does not have to rely on the judgment of one individual, has experts trained solely for the purpose of trust administration, and is under close governmental supervision.

The field of trusts is an extremely complicated one. Expert advice is essential. Suffice it to say that by the intelligent use of trusts you can effect very substantial estate and income tax savings. You can transfer income from your high bracket to someone in a lower bracket. You can substantially reduce your taxable estate and your income taxes by putting property and income into an especially designed trust; however, definite conditions must be met in each instance.

Most banks that maintain trust departments are eager to supply you with information. Be sure, however, to be in close contact with your attorney so that any trust you may consider will coincide with your over-all estate plan. It must be noted that lawyers, similar to physicians, often specialize in one field of their profession. A specialist is needed for estate planning. If the experience of your attorney is limited in this field, ask him to associate an expert on your behalf, or ask your banker or insurance man to recommend one. You have too much at stake to depend on anyone less than expert.

Physicians in all income brackets need estate planning. The young doctor, new in practice, may want to consider his planned insurance program as an estate plan. As he progresses financially and/or his family grows, his need for estate planning becomes greater. The larger his estate, the more acute his need for proper planning. Estate planning usually results in peace of mind, safety of hard-earned assets, and tax savings worth many times its cost.

It is one of the most profitable investments you can make.

TABLE 10 ESTIMATED STATE AND FEDERAL ESTATE TAX AND ADMINISTRATION COSTS

Size of Taxable Estate	*Estimated Adm. Costs*	*Estate Tax Using Marital Deduct.*	*Estate Tax without Marital Deduct.*
$ 60,000	$ 4,300	—	—
120,000	5,800	—	$ 9,500
150,000	8,200	$ 1,050	17,900
200,000	9,750	4,800	32,700
300,000	15,400	17,900	62,700
500,000	25,500	47,700	126,500

35. *Family Insurance*

Coverage on the Wife and Children?

For many, many years, insurance policies have been available to cover the lives of women and children. The basic need for these policies pertained to the sudden financial setback caused by last expenses when a member of the family died. Many husbands insured their wives in order to be able to afford housekeeping help until such time as other arrangements for the care of the children could be made. Usually, policies bought on wives consisted of whole life or other forms of permanent coverage. Very often, a father bought educational endowments for his children as savings programs towards their education, as well as for death protection while they were under his wing.

Today, individual policies on wives and children can still be purchased. If the protection on the life of the wife is designed for housekeeper funds, permanent or term insurance on her life can be utilized. If the coverage is needed for tax or estate purposes, it becomes essential that permanent and individual insurance on the life of your wife be obtained. Her death, for example, would remove the advantage of the marital deduction in your estate plan and would thereby increase the estate tax that must be paid upon your death. This automatically decreases the total amount you would leave to your children. You could insure her life to make up this loss.

How much does the loss of the marital deduction mean to you in dollars and cents? (See table, page 155.)

The only way these losses can be covered adequately is by an individual permanent policy on your wife.

Unfortunately, there have been numerous occasions when fathers purchased expensive endowment policies for their families while they

Your Gross Estate less Expenses	*With Wife Alive*	*With Wife Dead*	*Loss*
$100,000	$100,000	$ 95,200	$ 4,800
120,000	120,000	110,500	9,500
150,000	148,950	132,100	16,850
200,000	195,200	167,300	27,900
300,000	282,100	237,300	44,800
500,000	452,300	373,500	78,800

themselves had inadequate coverage. This often created a situation wherein widows and orphans were left with expensive insurance policies on their own lives instead of bread and butter.

In order to correct this situation and, incidentally, to create an attractive selling package, the insurance industry, within the last few years, has devised a family plan. This includes all members of your family under one policy and usually is composed of the following coverages:

$5,000 of whole life on the father.
1,000 of term on the mother.
1,000 of term on each child and any future children.

This describes what is often referred to as one unit of family plan. Most companies limit you to a purchase of no more than three units, which would triple all figures listed.

The only portion of the family plan that builds equity is the coverage on your own life. The greatest percentage of the premium outlay is invested in a cash-value type of permanent insurance. Included in the plan is a benefit on your life, guarantying double the indemnity if your death is caused by an accident, and a disability provision under which the company waives all premiums while you are disabled. Furthermore, in the event of your death, the rest of the family remains insured without further premium payment until their coverage normally expires.

The amount of insurance on your wife varies with her age. It is one-fifth of your own if you and she are of equal ages. If she is older than you, she gets less coverage; if she is younger, she receives more coverage. Most family plans provide for the expiration of your wife's coverage in the year that you would have reached, or do reach, age sixty-five. At that time, your wife has the right to convert her amount of term coverage to any form of permanent insurance she desires. However, remember that this conversion must be made at a premium rate in effect at that older age and, in most cases, that premium is too prohibitive to be worth the conversion.

Your children's coverage usually remains in effect until they are twenty-one years of age. At that time, it either expires or they may convert their portion up to five times the original amount without evidence of insurability. Thus, if you have purchased two units of family plan, affording your children $2,000 worth of protection until age twenty-one, they may at that age convert to any permanent plan up to $10,000 without medical examination or regard to their occupations. Again, the premium paid upon conversion will be that which is in effect when the children are twenty-one years of age. This conversion benefit does provide a certain amount of safeguard against the possible uninsurability of your children. You guarantee that they will be able to obtain a minimum amount while they are still young. However, this should not be a great influencing factor in the purchase of a family plan, since it is rare that a person of twenty-one will find himself uninsurable.

The greatest benefit of the family plan lies in the fact that you can put most of the premium to work toward your own future retirement income and still obtain a certain measure of protection for your family at a very low cost. This eliminates the necessity of having to invest monies into permanent plans for children. Nevertheless, it would be wise to have some permanent coverage on your wife in addition to that provided by the family plan. Conversion at old age becomes prohibitive, yet, the need for last expense coverage always exists.

The family plan has become one of the most popular policies in the United States. Many men who would normally not be able to spread their premium dollars to insure several people purchase this plan. Most physicians, however, are not faced with severe financial hardship in the event of an untimely death of their wives or a child. They tend first to insure their own economic worths for their families and to invest available premiums toward that goal. Only when they are satisfied that their personal programs are adequate, do they purchase policies on their wives and children.

Beware of the mistake of cancelling insurance now in force on your life and replacing it with the family plan. In most instances, the additional benefits of the family's term coverage derived from this move are not worth the loss of equity and incontestability existing in your present insurance.

Several companies are now offering the same family coverage, but in the form of a rider attached to your permanent policy. Although the theory is the same, this is a much more advantageous arrangement since you have the freedom of choosing the base policy and amount most suitable to your needs. If you are interested in the additional family coverage, ask your agent if your company permits the addition of a family rider to an existing policy. Under this circumstance, the benefit might be an intelligent buy. If an addition is not permitted, you may have to purchase another policy on your life before this rider can be obtained.

Having completed their own estate programs, many physicians purchase whole life or other policies on their sons. This gives a boy a headstart in terms of lower premiums, insurability, and everincreasing cash equity. Often, a guaranteed insurability rider is used to assure the availability of additional policies in the future.* This can be a significant gesture on your part. It can provide monies when they are most needed, protection when it is essential, and may be the only coverage your son will ever be able to own.

* See Chapter 20, "Your Insurability—Pay Now—Buy Later."

36. *Disability Income—A Brief History*

The disability income phase of the insurance industry is still in its infancy. It is only since 1940 that broad, liberal, noncancellable disability income policies have emerged from a labyrinth of experimentation, disappointment, defeat, retreat, and shock.

The first successful form of disability coverage came to the United States when the Travelers Insurance Company was founded in 1863. The company issued accident policies with accidental death benefits and small accident income benefits payable for short durations. The lack of statistics based on experience made it impossible to progress other than slowly and conservatively.

Toward the end of the century, some companies began to grant sickness as well as accident benefits. Coverages became broader and more liberal. Companies granted this benefit to almost any applicant. Nothing had ever put this new coverage to a test. Then came the depression. Claims, honest and otherwise, were so severe that one major company actually became insolvent and had to be rescued through reorganization. Licking their financial wounds, most insurance companies either discontinued writing all disability income benefits, or devised policies based upon realistic reappraisals of the 40 years of feast and ten years of famine. Underwriting became very strict and conservative, safety factors were incorporated to protect the companies from a repetition of the disaster, and clients were carefully selected.

The last 22 years have seen a slow recovery of the industry. Statistics have been more carefully compiled and studied. Conservative acceptance of risks has been strictly adhered to. New policies have been devised to grant liberal benefits to those whose occupation, character, morals, health, and other factors warrant them. Enough safety elements, such as limits to the amount of coverage one company will issue, types of occupational groups that may be granted coverage, have been incorporated into disability policies to protect the companies' integrity with their policyholders, and to insure the healthy growth of this infant of the industry.

37. How a Disability Premium Is Established

"We consider all the necessary factors, take a calculated guess, look into a cloudy crystal ball, keep our fingers crossed and come up with a premium."

With only slight exaggeration, that is how your cost for a disability income policy is determined.

Disability is a vague concept altogether. The insurance companies are faced with a puzzling set of circumstances:

1. What may be disabling to one individual, may be only a nuisance to another. The loss of several fingers may disable a physician to a point where he is prevented from pursuing his profession; but to a salesman, it may only mean that he must carry his briefcase in his other hand.

2. An individual cannot fake death, but he can purposely prolong recovery from disability if he feels that it is profitable for him to do so. He may even arrange for a vacation with pay by causing a disability of minor severity to occur. This creates a moral hazard which is difficult to discover and even more difficult and embarrassing to be forced to prove.

3. A physical impairment or history may have little or no effect on longevity but usually serves as a source of future disabilities. By covering these probable losses, a company may be buying claims.

4. Individual background and environment can greatly influence the risk. A physician whose office is in a rough neighborhood may be mugged one evening, and disabled for a long time. An individual whose moral conduct leaves much to be desired is wading through an ever-swelling sea of trouble. A heavy drinker, a gambler, a speed

demon, all invite disabilities. Insurance companies try to weed out such adverse risks.

5. New drugs and improved medical procedures constantly throw past calculations out of focus. The crippler of yesterday is no longer a menace. On the other hand, although new medical treatments often save the patient who might formerly have succumbed, the illness still leaves him with some degree of permanent or recurring disability.

6. Since there are so many variable factors involved, no accurate or even nearly complete records are available on which to base anything other than an intelligent guess. Studies indicate that one set of probabilities applies to one group under one set of circumstances, while the variation of a single factor, such as past medical history, throws all calculations out of focus.

These are some of the problems that face a company when it tries to determine a disability premium.

Those companies selling policies which may be cancelled at their options have the opportunity to re-evaluate their activities each time the policies come up for renewal. If their calculated guess was wrong, they can cancel or amend policies to correct the error.

Companies writing group insurance policies fall into the same category, since they also are in a position to readjust or cancel coverage.

The guaranteed renewable policy limits the companies' actions to adjustment of premium only, but prevents cancellation.

The companies issuing disability income policies which are both noncancellable and guaranteed renewable must be most careful in their selection of risks. If they make miscalculations, they can neither cancel nor limit policies, nor can they raise premiums. Their premiums are, therefore, generally higher in order to prepare for the financial shock of claims which will occur, especially in the older ages, and which they are legally and morally bound to honor fully, again and again.

The keys to the determination of a premium are:

1. The frequency of loss. How often are certain men, of a certain age, in a certain occupation, of a certain background, and enjoying good health likely to be disabled?

2. The severity of loss. How long are these men usually disabled?

3. Amount of coverage. How much will they have to be paid?
4. Type of coverage. For how long will they have to be paid?

These four questions can only be thought of as the probability of loss—the theory. Enough funds must be available to pay the actual loss—the experience.

Most companies must charge you a premium that enable them to set up several reserve funds in order to meet all obligations. The interest these reserve funds earn helps to reduce the necessary premium.

Allowances must also be made for the operating expenses of the company.

The disability insurance industry is eagerly compiling data and devising statistics which someday may be as accurate as those pertaining to mortality statistics which are used to determine your life insurance premium. Until then, the industry does the best it can and keeps its mental fingers tightly crossed.

38. *Should You Own Disability Income?*

You, at work, are probably worth more than $600,000 to your family. If you are age thirty-five, and your net income over the next 30 years will average no more than $20,000 per year, you will have earned $600,000 by the time you retire.

This money will have bought you a comfortable home, will have fed and clothed your family, will have educated your children, will have pumped a small fortune into your local economy for goods and services and, indirectly, will have maintained jobs for your patients.

You probably own enough life insurance to compensate for the tremendous financial loss your death would incur for your family. They must go on living and spending. Yet, what greater disaster can face a father and husband than being disabled without income, and watching lifelong savings and assets dwindle while his family tightens the belt? Economically speaking, your family would be better off if you sustained an actual death. At least, the income provided by life insurance would be available. Disability, however, is a living death. "The difference between the living death and the actual death is only six feet of sod," says Dr. S. S. Huebner, often called "the father of the life insurance industry."

As a physician, you have no company benefits, governmental assistance, or pension plans to provide income while you are disabled. You must, therefore, rely on your own devices to set up a method of continuing income during such period of adversity.

Painstaking studies indicate that the physician faces living death more often than actual death. The Society of Actuaries reported in

1952 that almost one-third of one thousand men aged thirty-five will suffer a disability of three months or longer before they reach age sixty-five. The average length of disability will be somewhat over four years. The odds that a long-term disability, rather than death, will strike at any given age were discovered to be as follows:

Age	*Chances of long-term disabilty rather than death*	*Average duration of long-term disability (3 mos. or more)*
30	2.7 to 1	4 years
40	2.3 to 1	4½ years
50	1.8 to 1	5½ years
59	1.6 to 1	6½ years

Quality disability income protection is designed to replace your basic income so that life at home can continue. Without such coverage, your assets and reserves which were painfully accumulated, after heavy taxes, over a period of years must eventually be exhausted. Few physicians have enough reserves to sustain their home obligations for a long period of time. In many cases, you may have to borrow the cash equities from your life insurance to satisfy family needs. This action reduces the death benefit of your insurance at the very time you need it most.

Disability income protection enables you to retain your reserves, keep your life insurance in full effect, and have peace of mind. The knowledge that a disability will not bankrupt your family permits you to devote full mind and energy to your practice.

Life and disability insurance go hand in hand. Both are indispensable to your welfare.

Your income is the producer of home, food, clothing, education, car, entertainment, luxury, and all other tangible items which contribute to your individual way of life. It is the goose that lays the golden egg. Keep the goose insured!

39. *Disability Income*

How Much and What Kind Should You Own?

Children don't care how you pay for their food. They eat heartily whether you earn money in a medical practice, an investment office, a shoeshine parlor, or at the race track.

Since your income depends upon your ability to practice medicine, you must provide a replacement of that income when you lose that ability for any length of time.

That ability to earn represents a sizeable economic value to your family. If you average $25,000 a year, starting with age thirty-five, by the time you are sixty-five you will have produced three-quarters of a million dollars of income. Would you insure a building of such value for $12,000? Yet, if your disability income program consists of a policy which pays $500 a month for two years of sickness, you are insuring your economic value for $12,000.

Your earnings actually exceed your minimum requirements for survival. Out of this excess, you purchase your luxuries. But when you are disabled, luxuries are soon forgotten.

You should have enough disability income to cover at least your basic family and home obligations for a long time. Keep in mind that during disability you will not only cease to be a producer of income, but you will become a heavy consumer of special goods and services, not normally required.

A disability of short duration usually does not upset your standard of living radically. A prolonged disability, on the other hand, often forces you to readjust your living standard downward in order to survive without becoming a pauper. The longer you are disabled, the more adept you must become at managing your dwindling finances; frugality becomes essential.

Don't sell your family short by forcing their standard of living into an abyss, when you become disabled, because you did not provide enough income. Don't sell yourself short by cutting off all disability income too soon.

Just as a planned life insurance program normally provides more coverage while your children are totally dependent and less coverage in later years, so should your disability income coverage be programmed to face economic reality.

Let us assume that you need at least $1,000 a month to maintain your family. It would be foolhardy to own only $400 a month of disability income. It would be equally as dangerous to own $1,000 a month of coverage which pays sickness benefits (which, by the way, represent 90 per cent of all claims) for only two years. On the other hand, it would be quite expensive and, because of company limitations, difficult to purchase $1,000 a month income with sickness benefits to age sixty-five.

In this case, the ideal program would provide for $1,000 a month for five years, $700 a month to the tenth year, and $500 a month to age sixty-five at which time the cash values of your life insurance could supply income for the rest of your life.

Graphically, the program would look like this:

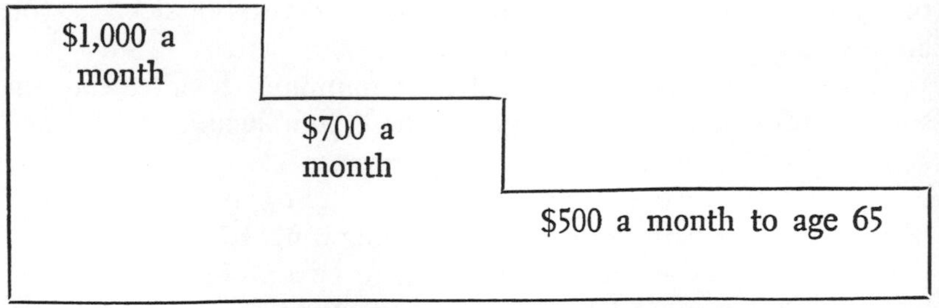

Total income replacement value, ages 35–65 = $222,000

This type of program would help you and your family to adjust yourselves slowly, knowing what the future holds financially.

You should utilize whatever premium you can afford to insure against the most devastating of all risks: a prolonged or chronic disability. Long-term coverage automatically covers short-term disabilities, but short-term coverage will fail you during long-term disability.

Arrange your disability income coverage with as much care as you do your life insurance program. You can only die physically once—but you can suffer economic death several times in a lifetime. During prolonged disability you will be there to witness the family's distress, which can be prevented by intelligent planning.

40. *Definition of Disability*

While Crossing an Open Field Fenced in on Three Sides . . .

Draw up a disability policy containing any benefits you desire, such as $1,000 a month income from the first day for life, no restrictions of any kind, and at a premium cost of $10 per year. Throw in any other benefits you want. Then, include as the definition of disability the following clause:

> The insured will be considered disabled if he is injured while crossing an open field fenced in on three sides, and hit by a bull on the right cheek on a Thursday morning, with a full moon shining brightly over his left shoulder.

How valuable is the rest of the contract?

Obviously, the example cited above is a bit overdone; but the wording of the definition can make yours either a dependable policy or a future cause for litigation and heartache.

There are four basic definitions and several combinations and variations of these in today's disability policies. Your present contract considers you disabled under one of the following four circumstances:

1. You are unable to engage in any occupation for remuneration or profit. This is the usual definition used in disability riders attached to life insurance policies. You must, virtually, be a vegetable in order to collect benefits, since your ability to earn any amount of money in any way ends your disability payments.

2. You are unable to engage in any occupation for which you are reasonably fitted. This definition at least recognizes that, as a

physician, you should not be expected to peddle newspapers. Yet, the weakness lies in the fact that if you do engage in anything to earn some money after being disabled, you must obviously be fitted for it or you would not be doing it.

3. You are unable to engage in any occupation in which you are reasonably fitted by training, background, and experience. This is much more liberal than the previous definitions. Your status as a professional man is recognized. You would not be considered ineligible for benefits if, for example, you became a cashier in your brother's restaurant while rehabilitating after a disability.

4. You are unable to perform the regular duties of your profession for a period of one, two, three, or five years. If you are still disabled at the ends of the years stated, the definition changes to one of the three discussed earlier. This is the most liberal definition. As a physician, you should own a policy containing it. The impact can be clearly shown by this example:

Suppose a surgeon became disabled. His surgical practice was finished. He would receive disability payments for the number of years stipulated, even though he might decide to become a pharmaceutical detail man and be earning a fair living at it. He might become medical director of an insurance company. He might become a full-time instructor at a medical school. Having been insured in his own occupation, he would continue to receive payments. After the stipulated years were over, the insurance company would determine if the rehabilitated doctor were entitled to further benefits under the second part of the definition. Although most physicians would certainly be doing something for which they were fitted at that point, they are at least assured of income long enough to be able to establish a new financial existence.

One policy even liberalizes the second portion of the definition to include the words "training, background, and prior economic status." The owner of this particular policy will be insured in his own occupation for five years. After this length of time, if he still cannot practice medicine but is engaged in an occupation related to his training and background, this insuror would continue to make payments, provided the income from the insured's new occupation was still well below what he earned as a physician. Although no definite amounts or percentages are mentioned, the intent of that company is clear.

During recent years, the courts have placed liberal interpretations on definitions, in favor of the physician. Many have received benefits although they had weak contracts. But they did have to go to court. A good definition in a good contract assures you of dependable income without a court fight and without the expenses and heartache such action brings.

DEFINITIONS (paraphrased) OF DISABILITY LISTED IN ORDER OF QUALITY

1. Insured as a physician for five years, and thereafter if you are unable to engage in any occupation in which you can reasonably be expected to engage, having due regard for training, background, and prior economic status.
2. Insured as a physician for five years, and thereafter if you are unable to engage in any occupation for which you are reasonably fitted by training and experience or achievement.
3. Insured as a physician for five years, and thereafter if you are unable to engage in any occupation for which you are reasonably fitted.
4. Insured as a physician for one, two, or three years, and thereafter if you are unable to engage in any occupation for which you are reasonably fitted by training and experience.
5. Insured as a physician for one, two, or three years, and thereafter if you are unable to engage in any occupation for which you are reasonably fitted.
6. If you are unable to engage in any occupation for which you are reasonably fitted by training and experience.
7. If you are unable to engage in any occupation for which you are reasonably fitted.
8. If you are unable to engage in any occupation for gain or profit.

Beware of misleading definitions which seem to insure you in your own occupation, but really mean you may not engage in any. For example, it may read:

"Insured as a physician for two years if unable to engage in his own or any other occupation."

In effect this means that you are covered only if you are unable to engage in any occupation whatever. Under this tricky wording you could not, for instance, accept a teaching post during a period of rehabilitation.

41. *Standard Provisions*

What You Can Expect To Find in Your Disability Policy

The Eskimo was bewildered by civilization. However, he took things pretty much in stride. He had paid $200 to Honest Joe at the "Top o'the Hill Used Car Lot" for a contraption they called a car. The ride downhill was a bit frightening but fun.

The car rolled to a halt. The Eskimo was perplexed. No matter how hard he pressed the accelerator, the car did not move.

A helpful stranger jerked open the hood.

"Hey, fellow," he exclaimed, "Where's your motor?"

The Eskimo was puzzled.

"Motor?" he mused. "Was there supposed to be one?"

Similar to life insurance policies, all disability income contracts contain certain standard provisions; some of these can greatly influence your future. It is essential that you be able to spot the key provisions. Only then can you determine if you have a quality contract.

Somewhere in your policy, you should be able to find these vital benefits. The omission of any indicates lack of coverage on the point or points omitted. If certain ailments are specifically listed, it indicates that those not mentioned are not covered. Although not necessarily in the order shown, here are the provisions you will find in your policy:

1. On the top or bottom of the first page you will find a statement which may proclaim your contract to be noncancellable and guaranteed renewable to your age sixty-five. On the other hand, it may state that renewal is at the option of the company. Some policies may

use evasive phraseology such as "may not be cancelled unless all policies of the same series are cancelled," "may not be cancelled but premiums may be adjusted from time to time," or "noncancellable for the period for which premiums are paid."

As far as you are concerned, you either own the policy at your present premium (noncancellable and guaranteed renewable) or you rent it from the company as long as it feels it is profitable to renew your "lease."

2. One section deals with definitions.

a. "Accident" should be defined as "bodily injury" and should not include the phrase "accidental means." The former indicates that you will be paid for any injury, regardless of its cause. The latter refers only to those injuries toward which you contributed in no manner whatever. If a heavy box you were lifting broke your toes, the accident could easily be interpreted as having been caused by a voluntary action on your part and, under "accidental means," could cause you to lose benefits.

b. Sickness should be defined as "any illness or disease originating while the policy is in force."

c. Another provision should state that once the policy has been in force for two years, it is incontestable regarding any statements in the original application and regarding your physical condition at the time of the application. Furthermore, any sickness beginning after the two-year contestable period has expired should be fully covered, no matter when it may have originated. This will protect you if a disease, of which you were not aware at the time of application, disables you in later years.

d. Disability should be clearly defined. Since this is the most important section of your policy, a detailed chapter, 40, "Definition of Disability" is devoted to it.

3. The waiver of premium clause will indicate when the company will take over your premium payments during disability. Most quality contracts call for 90 consecutive days of disability before premiums are waived.

4. Other provisions include:

a. Length of coverage for accident and sickness.

b. Commencement of coverage.

c. Partial Disability. This is a statement of the company's interpretation of partial disability; if you will be paid for disability resulting from both accident and sickness, and for how long this benefit is payable.

d. Blindness and Dismemberment. Many policies consider you totally disabled under these conditions. Some will limit benefits if either is caused by sickness rather than accident. Others provide lump sum payments in lieu of, or in addition to, other benefits.

e. Recurring Disability. Most companies will recognize any disability which recurs, after you have returned to practice for at least six months, as a new disability for which all benefits begin over again. Thus, if you have a five-year sickness benefit, are disabled for four years, return to the practice for over six months and are again disabled by the same illness, your five-year benefit period starts over again.

f. Exceptions or Reductions. This section spells out the conditions under which you are not covered. This usually includes suicide attempts, private piloting and military aviation, war and military service, foreign travel restrictions, and some other risks.

g. Claim Procedure. Requirements are listed pertaining to reporting a claim, actions that must be taken by both you and the company, and rights of physical examination granted to the company. The most important point for you to remember is to report a disability within 20 days of its occurrence. Usually, a phone call or letter to the agent or local office is considered notification. A quality company will take over from that point, supply you with proper forms and assistance to fill them out, and will pay your benefits promptly and courteously.

h. In the event your age had been misstated on the application, you would receive those benefits which your premium would have bought at your correct age.

i. Most policies state that your benefits and premiums will not be adjusted and coverage will remain in effect if you change to a more dangerous occupation or even temporarily engage in a perilous venture.

j. Some contracts use the average earnings or insurance related to earnings clause. This limits your benefits under certain circumstances. A detailed chapter, 48, "The Average Earnings Clause," is devoted to this disadvantageous clause.

k. Methods of reinstatement of a lapsed policy, grace periods allowed for premium payment, exact premium, renewal dates, and other procedural clauses are found in all policies.

In most cases, the policy which has a liberal definition of disability, is noncancellable and guaranteed renewable, and defines its terms clearly is a quality contract. It reflects its liberality in the rest of the standard provisions. A company which issues a quality policy is most anxious to pay all legitimate claims promptly. It knows that one dissatisfied client can destroy the reputation of integrity which it has been building over decades. A quality company cares how you react to its contract and service.

A good disability income policy may cost a bit more than the average, but the peace of mind it affords and its dependability in time of need are well worth the price.

42. *Standard Exclusions*

What Will Your Disability Income Policy Not Cover?

A good insurance man will always point out all provisions in his policy. After all, he wants you to know exactly what coverage you would or would not receive.

All disability income plans have certain exclusions. They are written into the policy, not only to limit the company's risk under specific circumstances, but also to define limitations clearly so that the company may avoid future litigation with you.

These are the standard exclusions:

1. Intentionally self-inflicted injury, such as suicide attempts.

2. Disability resulting from declared or undeclared war.

3. Military flying or the use of an aircraft for reasons other than transportation, such as racing, testing, or skywriting. Some policies exclude all disabilities related to aviation except those incurred as a fare-paying passenger on a scheduled airliner. The application for disability insurance specifically asks about flying activity. If you are a private pilot at the time of application, you will most likely receive a policy which excludes such aviation. However, some companies will grant full coverage for an additional premium. In most cases you must have a certain minimum number of hours in the air in order to receive any aviation coverage, even at an additional premium. These same companies will waive the additional premium after you have logged one hundred hours or more. Individual company practices govern in each case. If there is no specific exclusion of private flying, you will be covered for it even if you become a pilot after your policy has been issued.

4. Prior Origin of Disability. Most policies do not cover injury

or sickness originating before the policy was issued. However, once the policy is two years old, it becomes incontestable, and disabilities will be considered as having originated after the date of the policy. This protects the company against the occasional attempt by the client to defraud, but, on the other hand, protects you against the occasional attempt by a company to blame a disability on a condition existing many years ago; a condition of which you may not even have been aware.

5. Foreign Travel. Many companies automatically cover you for six months while you are in a foreign nation. If you intend to remain out of the country longer than six months, you must notify the company. If the country in which you are temporarily residing is a civilized one, coverage will be promptly verified. Otherwise, you may be charged an additional premium or coverage may be suspended altogether until you return. The greater the increase in risk due to your travels, the more conservative is the action of the company.

Some companies require notification whenever you leave the borders of the United States, Mexico, or Canada. In today's age of jet passenger service, it is quite possible for you to be back at the office, after a delightful, long week end in Paris, before your insurance company issues a travel rider for the trip. If your policy contains the automatic six-month coverage, it solves the problem conveniently. A few of the large companies, although granting this automatic coverage, specifically state that they will not pay benefits beyond six months if you are then still out of the country. This can make you a very unhappy man if you are in a foreign hospital with a broken back.

6. Disability due to inguinal, umbilical, or postoperative hernia is considered under the sickness provisions. Bacterial infections are considered under sickness benefits, except for pyogenic infections incurred through an accidental wound.

"What's the difference how they consider it?" you might ask. Were the foregoing considered accidental, benefits would usually begin from the first day and continue for as long as you were disabled. Under the sickness provision, however, the company usually begins benefits after a waiting period, anywhere from 8 to 30 days, and limits payments to a stipulated length of time.

In addition to these standard exclusions, some policies may also specifically exclude disabilities caused by mental illness or neurasthenia, by use of narcotics or intoxicants, or by venereal disease. Others will limit their risks by considering as sickness any accident where bodily or mental infirmities are contributing factors, any surgical or medical accidents, blood poisoning, heat prostration, fungus infections, or ptomaines.

Still others will only cover heart disease, cancer, and female disorders originating after the policy was at least six months old.

The integrity of a company is often indicated by the number of exclusions in its policies and by the clarity, or lack of clarity, and wording of these provisions.

If, at the time of application, you have a history of poor health, the company will probably exclude any disability caused specifically by the previously existing condition. If this exclusion is clearly stated, it indicates that you will be covered for all other future ailments. But how would you react to such an exclusion if it read "will not cover any disability due to disorders of the circulatory system"? A company anxious enough to deny a costly and seemingly questionable claim can often attribute many ailments to a disorder of the vast circulatory system.

Keep in mind that many special exclusions due to health history can be removed in later years, if you experience no recurrence.*

Own a policy with as few exclusions or limitations as possible. What may appear at the time of purchase as an unimportant and farfetched restriction, can become a source of anguish and litigation in the future. When you are disabled, you cannot afford to fight in the courts.

* See Chapter 21, "The Special Risk."

43. *Noncancellable Coverage*

Own—Don't Rent

Would you invest in office equipment, furniture, and stationery and then sign a lease which reads: "This ten year lease may be cancelled by the landlord at any time"? If your disability policy contains the phrase "This policy is renewable at the option of the company," you rent but do not own the protection. It can be taken from you at any time.

The physician is in an enviable position today, inasmuch as he can obtain noncancellable and guaranteed renewable coverage. This means that his policy cannot be cancelled by the company, restrictive riders or limitations cannot be placed on his policy once it has been issued, his benefits and coverages cannot be changed due to a change of occupation or state of health, and his premium is guaranteed and cannot be raised for any reason. Most noncancellable and guaranteed renewable policies expire at age sixty-five. Some contain provisions whereby you may continue the policy with the consent of the company after age sixty-five.

Make sure that your policy contains the words "noncancellable" as well as "guaranteed renewable." Some policies, unfortunately, refer to one or the other and thereby give a misleading impression.

If only noncancellable is mentioned, it usually means that the policy cannot be cancelled during the time that a premium has been paid. If, therefore, you pay your premium semiannually, the policy is safe from cancellation for the balance of the six months until the next premium is due. Obviously, this is not a noncancellable policy within the meaning discussed here. If a policy only mentions "guaranteed renewable," it usually means that you may renew the policy, but the company reserves the right to change the premium if it finds a basis for it. Therefore, it is conceivable that although a policy is guaranteed renewable, the premiums can be made so unattractive as to induce you to cancel it yourself.

The importance of ownership of noncancellable and guaranteed renewable disability coverage cannot be overemphasized. Certainly, you would not purchase a life insurance policy in which the company reserves the right to cancel it whenever it so desires. By the same token, you should not own a disability policy giving the company the same right. Your first claim will always be paid. If, however, the prognosis is such that it indicates to the company's medical department that many future payments will have to be made, those policies that are cancellable most often will be cancelled. That is the reason why noncancellable coverage costs more. The company underwriting it must build up enough reserves to pay for the serious disabilities which they know are coming. They cannot avoid the risk.

Disability income is one form of security on which you must be able to depend. You should own all the noncancellable and guaranteed renewable coverage you can afford. There are instances when you must, because of financial reasons, limit yourself to a basic program of noncancellable and guaranteed renewable protection and supplement that with other forms of coverage, such as guaranteed renewable only or group franchise. Your aim, however, should be to bring your noncancellable and guaranteed renewable insurance to that level which you find to be essential to the survival of your family.

This is certainly one time when you must shop for quality, not price.

44. *Issue and Participation Limits*

There Is a Limit to How Much You Can Buy

Regardless of how much you are willing to pay for it, you can own only a certain amount of disability income insurance. Each company limits the amount it will issue to you and the extent of its participation in your over-all disability insurance program. The companies recognize that a danger exists in insuring an individual beyond a certain limit and in providing him with too many tax-free dollars. This, they feel, removes his incentive to return to work, no matter what his earned income may be. Let us discuss issue limits for a moment.

Most companies today will issue no more than $500 per month disability income to a professional man. If you need $800 per month, you must therefore go to at least two companies in order to obtain it. Furthermore, all companies insist that your total coverage may not exceed 50 to 75 per cent of your earnings.

Let us discuss participation limits in detail. Each company will participate only to a certain extent in your over-all disability insurance picture. For example, let us assume that company A's participation limits are $600 per month. If you already own $200 per month when you apply to company A, this company will issue no more than an additional $400 per month. Company B's participation limits may be $800 per month. Thus, if you desire to have $800 per month coverage but already own $200 per month, you can obtain a second policy from company A of $400 to bring you up to $600, and after that has been issued, you may obtain another policy from company B in the amount of $200 per month, which will bring your total to $800. Once the second policy is in force, the company is not concerned about the new coverage that you subsequently bought.

The impact of this participation limit at a time of disability can be tremendous. To illustrate, let us take the hypothetical case of Dr. Benson.

This doctor recently applied for, and received, a disability income policy which will pay him $300 per month for accident or sickness. On the application, Dr. Benson stated that he already owned $200 per month with company A, and $300 per month with company B, for a total of $500 per month. The company to which Dr. Benson applied has a participation limit of $800. For that reason, he was able to get an additional $300 of noncancellable, guaranteed renewable income coverage. Unfortunately, the doctor neglected to mention the fact that he also owns $100 per week ($400 a month) of disability income through his medical association. Soon after the policy was issued, Dr. Benson was disabled with a cardial infarction. All companies paid him benefits without question except the one to whom he had recently applied. That company cancelled the noncancellable contract because had Dr. Benson mentioned his group insurance, the company would not have issued any policy; its participation limits would have been exceeded. Thus, Dr. Benson committed technical fraud by not reporting the group coverage. The company, during the contestable period, denied any liability.

Many physicians are unaware of participation limits. Yet, if these are not abided by, trouble can develop at claim time.

A perfect program should resemble the following:

Ficticious Company	*Participation Limit*	*Date Policy Effective*	*Amount of Coverage*
Reliable	$ 500	7–19–45	$300
Everlasting	600	3–19–46	300
Patriotic	800	4–21–47	200
Powerful	1,100	8– 8–49	300
State Medic. Society	2,000	10– 1–49	500
Natl. Medic. Society	2,000	3–25–51	400

Arranged in this order, the physician is able to build a disability income program of $2,000 per month without overstepping the participation limit of any company involved. At claim time, he will have no difficulty at all.

To safeguard your future security concerning participation limits, check your policies carefully. Each policy shows a date on which the insurance became effective. Classify these in the order in which they became effective. You may wish to contact your agent or company and inquire as to the particular company's participation limits.

It should be noted that in many instances companies differentiate between long- and short-term coverage, permitting larger limits of participation for short-term coverage. Usually short-term refers to sickness coverage which does not exceed five years of benefits, and long-term refers to sickness coverage of five years or longer. Furthermore, some companies consider group insurance as full coverage when considering participation, while others count it as half. In the latter case, $400 a month with a group would be figured as $200 per month for purposes of determining limits of participation.

It is strongly recommended that if in doubt, you contact your agent or company to ascertain your company's particular position in the matter of participation limits. This important item must be straightened out before claim time.

45. *Elimination Periods*

You Must Share the Risk

The cost of disability income protection would skyrocket if your insurance company were forced to put its claims and administrative procedures into operation every time you took a day off because of an upset stomach. It would cost them more to process your claim than you would receive. That is why the elimination period was devised.

Elimination period can be defined as a self-insuring period. Almost all disability income policies have provisions stipulating that benefit payments shall begin after the policyholder has been ill for a certain length of time. For example, you can purchase a policy calling for the insurance company to pay sickness and accident benefits beginning with the seventh, fourteenth, or thirtieth day of disability. Combinations, too, can be obtained. For example, you may purchase a policy which will pay accident benefits from the first day and sickness benefits from the thirtieth day. Most major insurors, however, will not pay sickness benefits from the first day. In order to eliminate piddling claims, almost all major companies require that you self-insure for at least seven days for disabilities due to sickness. First day accident coverage, however, is almost universal. Usually, an accident will be severe enough to disable you for longer than just a day or two, whereas a cold or an upset stomach would not.

How do these elimination periods affect you?

They enable you to tailor-make a program in accordance with your own needs. If, for example, you have ample funds to carry yourself for a 30-day period comfortably, you are able to reduce your premium by purchasing a policy with a 30-day self-insuring period.

If your medical partnership agreement calls for full income for the first 90 days of disability, half income for another period of time, thereafter followed by no income at all, a disability policy calling for a 90-day self-insuring period would be ideal. Why pay the premium for the first 90 days, during which your income will not be affected? If you are in private practice and your resources are such that you would not be able to carry yourself for any length of time, a self-insuring period of seven or 14 days in the event of sickness may be ideal. It must be remembered that almost all companies will be happy to lengthen the self-insuring period at a later date but few companies will want to shorten it. By lengthening the self-insuring period, the company actually assumes less of a risk and, therefore, will not hesitate to cooperate. On the other hand, by changing a self-insuring period from 90 to seven days, it is assuming a greater risk and will require either evidence of insurability or that a new policy be issued as of your age at the time of the change. Furthermore, you must remember that with a long self-insuring period you may have many short disabilities and never collect on any of them. For example, if you have a 60-day elimination period, you may have several disabilities lasting only 40 days and receive payment for none. You may also have a disability lasting 63 days for which you will receive only three days of benefit.

As you can see, it will require careful thought and intelligent counseling for you to determine which elimination period is most suitable for your particular situation.

Use Short Elimination Periods If:

1. You do not have large reserves to fall back upon.
2. You can afford the higher premiums required for short elimination periods.

Use Long Elimination Periods If:

1. You have ample reserves to sustain you for short-term disability.
2. You have a partnership or other agreement guarantying your income.

3. You wish to save on premiums.

4. You are not concerned about short disabilities, but would rather use the premiums saved to purchase a larger amount of coverage.

46. *Length of Sickness Coverage*

Don't Cut the Board Too Short!

How long will you be sick? If you can answer this question, you need not read on. You'll know exactly which policy to buy.

It is in the length of sickness coverage that most disability policies differ. Most of them grant lifetime income benefits if the disability is caused by an accident. Since it is the greater of the two risks, sickness coverage will be limited. Coverage for each sickness is available today for one, two, three, five, or ten years, and to age sixty-five. Obviously, the longer the sickness coverage, the higher the premium. It is not wise to choose sickness coverage of a short duration because it will cover only minor disabilities and will leave you deserted during major ones. Many experienced advisors insist that you should own the longest sickness coverage available. Others argue that in the event of a serious disability, you will certainly have either recovered or died within a ten-year period. Obviously, there is no pat answer to this problem.

There are numerous sicknesses which can prevent a physician from continuing his practice without immediately affecting his longevity. Glaucoma, for example, can certainly disable without killing.

The best way to protect yourself during the serious and lengthy illness and at the same time cover one of short duration is to own at least part of your sickness coverage with income payable to age sixty-five.

If a premium-paying problem exists, the question arises as to whether you should invest your premium dollars in long-term sickness coverage for a small amount of income or in short-term sickness coverage for a more adequate amount of income. For example, at age thirty-five you must pay $250 per year for a policy providing two-year sickness coverage at the rate of $500 per month. The same premium would buy ten-year sickness coverage providing $350 per month. This question can best be resolved by compromise. Certainly, family survival comes first. If it takes a certain number of dollars each month to feed the wife and children, that amount must be provided for, regardless of the length of the coverage involved. On the other hand, if a disability becomes a serious one and your total income is eventually cut off, it could mean financial ruin. A compromise would call for the purchase of some five- or ten-year sickness protection, supplemented by as much of short-term coverage as finances would permit. You should resolve, however, to obtain additional long-term sickness protection at the earliest possible date.

Your earning ability over a normal life span is worth a fortune. Only long-term sickness coverage can compensate you and your family for the loss of that fortune when you are disabled.

TABLE 11 YOUR POTENTIAL EARNINGS TO AGE 65

If your monthly earnings are:

Age:	*$800*	*$1,000*	*$1,500*	*$2,000*
29	$345,600	$432,000	$648,000	$864,000
35	288,000	360,000	540,000	720,000
41	230,400	288,000	432,000	576,000
47	172,800	216,000	324,000	432,000
53	115,200	144,000	216,000	288,000

47. *Recurring Disability*

What About the Second Heart Attack?

Dr. Benson could not endure the boredom. He would go back to the office, he thought, and limit his activity to a few patients a day. Disabled or not, he had to make an attempt at getting back to work. He was feeling much better, anyway. The disability insurance checks would stop, to be sure, but Dr. Benson was confident he could earn enough to compensate for this. The boredom, . . . he had to get back into action!

At first, the patient load was light. Dr. Benson felt fine. Slowly, his activities increased. At the end of three months, his waiting room again enjoyed heavy traffic.

The second attack struck suddenly. A screaming siren, concerned colleagues, oxygen, drugs; several weeks later, Dr. Benson was back at home—this time, however, not bored but worried. His insurance company had regretfully notified him that it could no longer make further disability income payments, since his return to work signified an end to his disability and, with it, an end to the company's obligation.

Claims statistics dealing with disability clearly indicate that the heaviest and most frequent benefits are paid to policyholders disabled by chronic and recurring illnesses. Following a serious disablement, you usually have lost your health to some degree. The damage has been done. The human machinery has been weakened and will probably break down again.

A quality disability income policy recognizes this problem. A provision is included which continues benefits if yours is a recurring disability. If you return to practice but are stricken again within six months, this recurrence is considered a continuation of the original disability. Suppose your policy calls for five years of sickness-disability payments and you return to the office after three years of disability. If you suffer a recurrence within six months, the company will continue your benefits for another two years. If, however, you have returned to your practice for longer than six months, a recurring illness is considered a new disability. Under the circumstances described, you would be entitled to another five years of benefits. Since the company extends coverage as if a new disability has occurred, you must also abide by whatever self-insuring period the policy requires for new disabilities. This may mean anywhere from eight to 90 days before benefits begin again.

Since the duration of the recurring disability is unknown, this is most certainly a small price to pay for renewal of full benefits for another five years. The recurring disability provision removes the penalty you might otherwise incur by attempting to resume your profession.

Without this provision, all benefits end as soon as you break the chain of continuous disability. You cannot afford to be without this important provision. Once your body has sustained a serious impairment, you can no longer obtain any policy to cover the inevitable recurrence of disability. Make absolutely certain your present contract has this built-in assurance of continued benefits.

48. *The Average Earnings Clause*

YOU MAY NOT GET WHAT YOU PAID FOR

"You get what you pay for," the saying goes. But this does not hold true for all disability income policies.

The average earnings or relation of earnings to insurance clause can be a most dangerous aspect of your disability insurance program. It gives the insurance company the right to pay you less than your policy promises if your earnings have been reduced prior to disability. If you earned $1,200 a month when you took out the policy and your total insurance coverage at that time amounted to $600 per month, you insured in a ratio of one to two, or one-half of your earnings. If the disability happens to occur during a depressive economic period when you are happy to average $600 a month income, some companies will pay you the same ratio on the current earnings, or $300 a month. They will return the portion of the premium you were charged for the larger amount of coverage during the two years immediately preceding your disability, but you will receive only half of what you expected.

Some insurance companies write this clause in order to protect themselves from the type of risk that would find it more profitable to be disabled than to be working. During the depression, many companies found that their disability departments went bankrupt. On the other hand, it seems unfair for a physician to pay a certain premium for insurance and then, if he is unlucky enough to be disabled at a time when his income has decreased, find that he receives less benefits than he has paid for. The return of the extra premium charge is small consolation for this disappointment. Be sure that your contract does not contain an average earnings or relation of earnings to insurance clause. There are excellent policies on the market today which do not contain this clause and there is no reason why any physician should own one that does.

Many companies that have included the average earnings clause in their policies are now beginning to write insurance without it. It may benefit you to check with your company to see whether this clause may be voided in your own contract.

49. *How Should You Pay Your Disability Premium?*

Let convenience be your guide.

That is the most practical way to determine how to pay for your disability income protection. Although it may cost a bit more to pay quarterly rather than annual premiums, the convenience of such intervals may be worth the price.

There are three reasons, however, why it would be most advantageous to pay premiums annually:

1. It is less expensive with most companies. Similar to life insurance, you pay an additional charge for modes other than annual. The extra charge is to compensate for the additional bookkeeping and administrative expenses involved.

2. Some companies will increase benefits 10 per cent if an annual premium method is used. Thus, if you need $800 per month, you only have to purchase $730 of coverage and pay annually. This increases benefits by 10 per cent ($73 a month) automatically and brings coverage up to $803 a month at a lower premium.

3. Regardless of these aforementioned points, the greatest advantage of annual premium payment deals with the waiver of premium benefit of your policy. This benefit usually guarantees that the company will not require premium payment if you are disabled longer than 90 days. The premium is waived as it falls due. If your premium becomes due on the ninety-first day of disability, for example, the company will credit you with it. If you are paying quarterly, they will credit you with a three month premium. Were you to recover a week later, you would have to resume premium payments at the next due date. If, however, you pay annually, they will waive a full

year's premium. You may recover and resume your practice a day or a week later; yet, you do not pay any premiums until a year later. In this way, you may pick up the value of a year's premiums.

All companies permit you to change the mode of premium payment. Whenever finances permit it, change yours to annual.

50. *Office Overhead Policy*

It Pays Your Office Expenses

Surely, you would not fire your aide, discontinue phone service, and lock your doors at the first sign of disability. You would keep your practice in operation as much as possible, with the help of your colleagues, so that your years of effort are not dissipated and so that you will have something to which to return.

Although your income is drastically reduced during disability, your office expenses continue.

A disability office overhead policy can be of great value to you. It pays your normal office expenses such as salaries, rent, utilities, while you are disabled. Payments can begin after 15 or 30 days of disability, and usually continue for one year. It is felt that if you are disabled that long, you will have to close your office or make other arrangements. By limiting the length of coverage realistically, the insurance companies keep the premiums low.

The objective of an office overhead policy can, of course, be attained by purchasing additional disability income coverage. However, there are several reasons why this may not be wise for you:

1. Since the amount of quality disability income coverage you are permitted to own is limited, you may fall short of your personal and home needs by diverting this valuable coverage for business and office needs.

2. The premium charged for office overhead insurance is much lower than that for personal noncancellable policies, since it provides coverage for only one year.

3. The premium for office overhead insurance is fully tax-deductible. Depending on your tax bracket, this lowers the cost even further. (The benefits, however, are taxable. Nevertheless, you will undoubt-

edly be in a lower tax bracket while disabled, and your office expenses are also tax-deductible. These can be considered compensating factors.)

4. You can build a substantial personal disability income program and still own office overhead coverage. Since this insurance is not direct income to you, almost all companies disregard it when they decide whether or not to participate in your over-all personal disability income program.

5. Many excellent overhead policies are available through medical associations and private insurance companies.

The sole practitioner finds it imperative to own such coverage for the continued operation of his office.

The medical partnership is faced with a different set of circumstances. Most partnership agreements make provisions for the continuation of the practice, on an equitable basis, during the disability of one of the partners. Even if no direct mention is made of a disabled partner's obligation to pay his share of expenses, he does so anyway if expenses are paid out of office income and accounts receivable. If, however, each partner owns an office overhead policy in the amount of his share of the office operation, the accounts receivable, from which his portion of the expenses no longer must be deducted, will be that much greater during his disability.

Medical associations are most interested in this form of protection. Many have made excellent arrangements for their members with the few insurance companies underwriting this policy on a group basis. These group plans, however, leave the door open for cancellation of the group by the insurance company. Recognizing the serious need and, incidentally, spotting a good opportunity for a "door-opener" to the medical market, more and more private companies are issuing office overhead policies which are guaranteed renewable to age sixty-five. Their premiums are, of course, somewhat higher than those of cancellable group plans.

Private companies reserve the right to adjust premiums of all policies at the same time, if claim experience necessitates such action. They must, however, renew your policy.

Association group plans also may adjust their premiums, but they may also cancel the whole group if and when they find it profitable to do so.

You should own guaranteed renewable coverage through a private company unless there exists a great difference in premiums or benefits between it and group plans. You can make this possible concession on the matter of cancellability, since the private plans can increase their premiums to a point where you would not want to renew anyway.

Someday, you will be able to purchase an office overhead policy which is noncancellable and guaranteed renewable and has a fixed premium. When that day arrives, you should incorporate such a policy into your disability program.

51. *The Medical Partnership and Disability*

Would you enter into a medical partnership with a one-armed surgeon?

Would you agree to share your income with a partner who spends every day on the sunny beaches of Miami and not in the office?

Would you be willing and able to support your partner's as well as your own family while he is on a two-year safari in India?

A disability can make your surgeon-partner into a one-armed practitioner overnight. A disability can force your partner to seek another climate for survival, leaving you to carry on as best as you can by yourself. A disability can put your partner out of action for several years. You cannot stand by without extending financial aid to which he and his family are legally and morally entitled. You certainly would expect the same attitude if you become the disabled partner.

Most partnership agreements, which form the legal foundation of the "professional marriage," are careful to protect the interest of his family when one of the partners dies. Few, however, make adequate and fair provisions for the much greater risk of prolonged disability.

One medical partnership tries to solve the problem by guaranteying the payment of the disabled partner's full share for three months. One half of the full share is then continued for an additional nine months. After this full year of disability, the stricken partner's share is reduced to 25 per cent for another six months. If he has not recovered by that time, the partnership is liquidated.

The results of this type of arrangement, although appearing practical and fair in the attorney's office, may not be so equitable at time of disability, regardless of whether you are the healthy or disabled partner.

The healthy partner must work much harder in order to maintain the practice and meet all expenses. In addition, he must support another family. Eventually, he may have to seek temporary assistance—another salary, another "mortgage" on accounts receivable.

Partnership business decisions must still be made with the disabled colleague. He may see things differently from where he sits—in a wheelchair.

Discontent is sure to follow, resulting in permanent damage to the partnership.

Now from the other point of view, the disabled partner is helpless. Although he will not suffer sharply for three months, he faces the prospect of reduced income for one-and-a-half years, and poverty thereafter. His personal expenses do not diminish after three months; they may even increase. He can no longer produce, only consume. His years in a labor of love have produced no factories with physical assets of great value that can be liquidated. His family's money-making machine has broken down. It will never again be in perfect repair.

The disabled partner understands that the practice cannot support him indefinitely, but the tremendous loss exists nevertheless.

How, then, can this problem be solved?

Business disability insurance, specified in the partnership agreement, can be of invaluable aid. This is the way it works:

1. The partnership purchases an office overhead disability policy in the amount of each physician's share of fixed expenses. The benefits usually last one year.* Premiums are tax-deductible as a business expense. This coverage automatically enhances the income of the practice during disability, since half of the expenses of maintaining the office will come from insurance rather than accounts receivable.

2. Each partner purchases a noncancellable, quality, disability income policy on the other partner. This should cover the greater risk of sickness for at least ten years, preferably to age sixty-five.

The insurance company can begin payments after a 60- to 90-day provision for full income from accounts receivable. This waiting period reduces the cost of the coverage and sets into motion an insurance program only in the event of a prolonged disability.

* See Chapter 51, "Office Overhead Policy—It Pays Your Office Expenses."

After a partner has been disabled for, perhaps, two years, during which time he has received a fair tax-free income, the healthy partner should buy him out for a preagreed price. The remaining eight years of disability benefits under the policy may well represent most of that purchase price. Partnership life insurance policies should be continued until the buy-out is completed. Should the disabled man die, the monies from this insurance will enable the survivor to complete his commitment to the deceased's family.

Under an insured arrangement such as this, the disabled partner receives a fair tax-free income promptly and regularly. The healthy partner can afford to obtain help, meet expenses, and fulfill a moral, as well as financial, obligation. Part of the eventual buy-out price is also available, thus easing the burden of meeting a sizeable sum from current earnings.

An apparent discrepancy of premium payments may exist if the partners are of widely separated ages. You must remember, however, that the older man is more likely to be disabled for a long period of time and you, the younger, may need the benefits to meet your obligations so much sooner.

Although the premiums for this coverage are not tax-deductible at this time, the benefits are tax-free. An $8,000 a year disability insurance program, for example, represents $16,000 a year of taxable income if you are in the 50 per cent bracket. This factor should be taken into consideration when you decide on an amount to be provided for partnership insurance.

Quality disability income policies can form the backbone of a sound partnership. The stronger the backbone, the firmer the stance.

52. *Group Insurance*

You May Be Left Holding the Bag!

August 15, 1962

Dear Dr. Benson:

Following a review of the XYZ Medical Association Group Insurance Plan, of which you are a member, it was concluded that this particular coverage should be discontinued as of the next premium renewal date. Of course, this is in harmony with Part J of the policy. Since this company is operated for its policyholders as a whole, we know you will agree that it is not fair for all to bear the excessive cost of one plan which is held by the minority. This action will have no effect on any pending applications for benefits which are payable under the terms of the policy.

If, at a later date, we are in a position to provide you with similar protection, you will be contacted by our local office. Your policy expires as of November 1, 1962.

Sincerely,

John X. Jones, V.P.
Dependable Life Ins. Co.
Greenville, Montana

October 21, 1962

Dear Dr. Benson:

We regret to advise that due to the apparent lack of interest evidenced by the insufficient number of applications received, the pro-

posed disability income plan offered by this company to replace your previous coverage did not become effective.

Sincerely yours,

Robert Z. Smith, V.P.
Everready Life Ins. Co.
Chicago, Ill.

Dr. Benson, uninsurable for personal coverage because of a recent coronary thrombosis, was left "holding the bag." He had always relied on group insurance through his association because the premiums were low. He had probably saved $600 to $1,000 in premiums over the last ten years, but now he would be willing to pay $1,000 for someone to give him noncancellable coverage.

The most glaring weakness of any group or association insurance lies in the fact that it can be cancelled at the option of the company or the administrators of the group. A group policy is a contract between the insuror and the professional association for the benefit of a third party, you, the individual. Cancellation affects all members of the association. Every time a claim is paid to any member of the group, it reduces the stability of your own policy. As the members grow older and claims become more frequent, the insurance company finds itself with greater losses and less than expected profits. At some point, the company will be forced to avail itself of the cancellation provision which was written into the contract for that contingency.

You should be aware of other important factors dealing with group insurance.

1. Usually the company undertaking to write the master policy for your association (you receive only a certificate showing that you are covered under the master policy), will stipulate the acceptance of uninsurable risks only if a certain percentage of all eligible members enroll. Experience has indicated that healthy physicians tend to replace most of their group coverages with personal protection as soon as they become financially able to do so, or after they have given the matter serious consideration. The uninsurable, however, clings to his group coverage for lack of an alternative. Under these

circumstances, when a group is cancelled, the next insuror will insist on enough of a majority of good risks to make the venture profitable. If you are the unfortunate bad risk, you may find yourself alone with your fellow uninsurables, composing the bulk of applicants. You will then receive the same letter that our troubled Dr. Benson received. He may be fictitious, but the letter was real.

2. Group insurance offers benefits by formula, not by individual needs. Amount and duration of coverage are limited to satisfy the requirements of the company, not you.

3. Your premium can be raised. Some master policies provide for premiums to be raised automatically when the members reach certain age brackets. Others quote a uniform premium for the life of the policy, but the company has the right to request more contributions. If these are not made, the group will be cancelled.

4. You have no voice in your program. You do not own your protection—you rent it. A change in the administration of your association could mean cancellation of the master policy by the new officers in favor of another insuror. The fact that few associations are ever found on the cancelling side of the picture does not preclude such occurrence.

5. You lose your insurance if and when you leave the group. You may find it advisable to relocate your practice in another section of the country. If you have meanwhile become uninsurable, you may not be able to replace the coverage when you settle in a new location.

6. Some group plans do not include the waiver of premium clause which takes over your premium payments while you are disabled. Many more will waive premiums only after you have been disabled for six months or longer, not the customary three months found in personally owned policies.

7. The law requires that companies issuing individual noncancellable disability policies must back up their insubvertible promises with substantial cash reserves. On group policies, however, no reserves are required. The company can always raise the premium or cancel the group altogether if the contract proves unprofitable.

8. Ownership of group disability policies can often prevent you from acquiring a personal program. There is a limit to how much coverage you can buy and, together with your group coverage, a pur-

chase of personal policies may bring you over that limit, and the desired protection may be refused.*

Why, then, do so many physicians own group disability insurance?

One reason is, undoubtedly, the attraction of the low premiums charged. This is sometimes adequate enough to cause them to rationalize away all unfavorable aspects. On the other hand, the low premium enables the young practitioner with limited income to obtain some coverage temporarily, until he can afford noncancellable and personally controlled policies.

Another reason may be the inability to purchase private coverage for reasons of health. Some physicians would be stranded without their group insurance.

A further reason may be the use of group insurance as a means of beefing up personal coverage. This is the primary intention of the various medical associations in making such policies available to their members. In this respect, group coverage can be of great advantage to the physician. By designating his higher cost noncancellable coverage for essential home needs, he can take the risk of covering less essential office and/or luxury needs with cancellable group policies.

The physician who is familiar with the weaknesses of group insurance will not make an error in judgment by depending solely on this type of coverage for disability income. Moreover, when he does purchase group policies as additions to his program, he will be fully aware of their limitations and will construct his program accordingly.

* See Chapter 44, "Issue and Participation Limits—There Is A Limit To How Much You Can Buy."

53. *Major Medical Insurance*

IT PAYS THE BIG MEDICAL BILLS

"I do own some hospitalization," remarked Dr. Benson, "but I am most concerned about a major illness or injury in the family. My cash reserves are limited, what with the new house and heavy expenses. Is there a policy which will jump to my aid during serious illness or injury?"

Yes, Dr. Benson can obtain a relatively new type of coverage called "major medical" or "catastrophe" insurance. It will assist him in times of such emergencies and help him to preserve the assets he may have spent years in accumulating.

As the name implies, major medical insurance is designed to relieve the terrible financial drain caused by serious illness or injury. Its basic construction is similar to that of your automobile collision policy.

Major medical plans contain a deductible feature of anywhere from $250 to $1,000. Before your major medical goes into effect, you must first have incurred expenses equal to the deductible amount, and incurred them, usually, within 90 days. The plan covers either 75 or 80 per cent of all expenses beyond the deductible called for, until the maximum of $5,000, $7,500, or $10,000 for each catastrophic occurrence has been paid.

Most policies provide for all benefits to start over again if the same illness recurs after 12 months, during which time you made no claim for it. Of course, claims for new ailments would be covered at once. Most policies also provide that there be only one deductible amount if more than one member of your family needs benefits at the same time because of the same injury. To illustrate, only one deductible amount need be sustained if an automobile accident causes serious injury to several members of your family.

Exclusions usually relate to pregnancy (unless complications arise), suicide attempts, war or military service, expenses covered by workman's compensation or occupational disease laws, cosmetic surgery not related to an injury, services supplied by U. S. Government hospitals, dentistry not occasioned by injury, alcoholism, mental disorders, and psychiatric treatment.

Before you purchase major medical, you should be aware of these points:

1. Major medical policies come in cancellable or guaranteed renewable forms. The cancellable type gives the company the right to discontinue the policy whenever it desires. The company can never deny a first claim, but if the prognosis is such that you would in the future become an unprofitable risk, the company may then cancel the policy.

The guaranteed renewable policy, on the other hand, takes the right of cancellation away from the company. Only you, by not paying your premium, can cancel your contract. There is, however, a hitch. If the experience of the company indicates that its over-all venture into the major medical field is not profitable, it may adjust the premium to compensate for unexpected losses. It cannot raise your premium alone, but can raise it on the basis of class (all class A risks, which includes doctors, dentists, lawyers), or on the basis of area (all policies in your state or section of the country), or on both.

So far, few companies have availed themselves of this privilege. One major insuror, finding itself with a major medical policy which offered too much to be profitable, simply discontinued issuance of this particular plan. Those who own the old policy continue to enjoy its liberal benefits; new clients, however, obtain another series of policies in which the premium and benefits have been adjusted to reflect the actual experience of that company.

2. Among guaranteed renewable policies, you will find variations in their termination dates.

a. Guaranteed renewable to age sixty-five. All coverage and premium payments end when you are sixty-five years of age.

b. Guaranteed renewable for life. You may continue the policy for as long as you live. You must also pay premiums for life.

Usually, this policy provides for either reduced total benefits after age sixty-five, or for an aggregate sum after that age. This means that if you are covered for $10,000 after age sixty-five and you have used up $5,000 by age sixty-seven, there is available another $5,000 to be utilized during your remaining lifetime.

c. Payable to age sixty-five, and then paid up. This contract is considered paid up at age sixty-five, but benefits continue on either a reduced or aggregate basis for life. Although a paid-up plan is slightly more expensive, it may best fit into your retirement plans. Your coverage would still exist, but you would have no premium outlay when retired and on a reduced income.

3. Your children may be covered to ages eighteen or twenty-five. At that point, they cease to come under your contract and must obtain their own.

4. Some policies guarantee your children the right to obtain their own major medical plans when their coverage under yours expires, regardless of their insurability at that time.

5. Your income may directly affect the deductible amount you may obtain. Some companies do not grant any major medical coverage to a family in which the combined gross income exceeds from $25,000 to $40,000 per year. Others will issue a policy to a high-income family only with $1,000 deductible.

6. Most policies will not permit you to own more than one form of major medical coverage. Others may not issue you a policy if you have unusually comprehensive hospitalization insurance.

7. Major medical covers expenses in or out of the hospital. There are policies on the market called major hospital. These pay only expenses incurred while you are hospitalized or when you require the full-time services of a registered nurse.

8. Many policies include limitations dealing with amounts to be paid for board, surgery, nursing services. Others may publish surgical schedules, similar to those found in hospitalization policies, with the intentions of limiting their contributions. Other stipulations may exclude for six months any operation or treatment of goiter, adenoids, tumors, or heart ailments. Any limitations of coverage should be carefully investigated.

9. The premium you must pay for major medical coverage will depend on your age (the ages of your wife and children are usually

immaterial), the coverage you will receive, its limitations, the guarantee of renewability and, of course, the experience of the issuing company.

Major medical is the most sensible type of health insurance. It affords the greatest potential benefits for the least premium.

As a physician, you may well be able to absorb a normal medical expense, but you are not immune to financial ruin if a serious illness or accident strikes. It can swiftly wipe out your reserves, can cruelly sink you into debt and obligation, and can destroy all your dreams for the future.

54. *Hospitalization*

Is It Really Necessary?

"It's helpful sometimes, but I can do just as well without it."

"Actually it's not real insurance. My premium certainly doesn't buy much of a risk."

"I am just trading dollars with the company. I can go on paying premiums for a while, then someone in the family has a short hospital stay and I get some of the money back."

"Since my colleagues extend professional courtesy, I sometimes make money on my hospitalization policy."

"I am not too much concerned about relatively minor hospital expenses. A serious illness or injury could hurt, though. That's why I don't have any hospitalization insurance. I used my premium dollars to get a good major medical plan."

"I carry Blue Cross and Blue Shield so that I don't have to be obligated to a colleague or hospital. I save a lot of money that way on gifts."

"Most of the hospitals in my home town discount the bills heavily for physicians or charge nothing at all. But I carry hospitalization anyway as a means of repaying the courtesy. Furthermore, it would help me if I had to go to a hospital in another city."

"I use my hospitalization policy to supplement my income while I am disabled. At $20 a day, I receive $140 a week which I can use as income if I don't need it to pay medical bills."

Opinion is sharply divided in insurance and medical circles as to the physician's actual need for hospitalization insurance. No one argues the fact that most families find this method of prepayment of medical expenses helpful. Many would find it difficult to save any money toward that purpose. But the physician often receives professional courtesy from colleagues and discounts from hospitals. His need for hospitalization is questionable. He can usually absorb relatively minor costs. Major medical coverage defrays large expenses.

Most insurance company hospitalization plans are similar in pattern. They provide benefits for:

Daily room and board—from $5 to $30 a day, from 30 to 365 days for each illness or injury.

Miscellaneous expenses—from $50 to $300.

Maternity—usually ten times the daily room rate.

Surgery—by schedule of operations, with a maximum of from $200 to $400 for the most serious.

There may be small additional benefits such as ambulance fees, outpatient accident allowances, polio coverages, and doctor's visits in the hospital.

Miscellaneous expenses may be unallocated, graded, or allocated.

If unallocated, the benefit provides for a certain amount to be paid toward any incidental expenses during any one illness or injury. It does not matter whether you were hospitalized for one or 60 days. The company will pay up to that stipulated amount for drugs, dressings, medicines, laboratory services, transfusions, x-rays, and anaesthetics.

If graded, the benefits provide for five times the daily room rate if you are hospitalized one day, six times for two days, and so on until it reaches 20 times for 16 or more days.

If allocated, the benefits are itemized. There may be an allowance of $15 for x-rays, $30 for blood transfusions, $10 for laboratory services, and so on. This is a most limited form of coverage. Few companies still use allocated miscellaneous benefits.

Surgery is covered in accordance with a schedule included in each policy. Major and minor operations are listed and the amount the company will pay for each surgical procedure is shown.

Maternity is usually covered if the baby is born at least ten months after the policy went into effect.

When you purchase a hospitalization policy from an insurance company, the contractual benefits remain the same no matter where you reside. Blue Cross benefits vary by state or region. Although you hold a contract in one state, you will receive the benefits provided in the state in which you are hospitalized. Even though you are a Florida resident, for example, you will receive the more liberal New York benefits if you are hospitalized in New York.

Most hospitalization policies do not cover admissions due to war, military service, suicide attempts, cosmetic surgery, and private aviation. They will not cover confinement in a free government hospital. Many policies exclude claims dealing with hernia, hemorrhoids, tonsils, adenoids, appendix, female reproductive organs, cancer, heart disease, and various other conditions until the policy has been in force for at least six months. Conditions existing prior to the purchase of the policy are usually excluded from coverage.

Very few hospitalization policies are truly noncancellable and guaranteed renewable with a fixed premium. Most policies can only be renewed with the consent of the company or association, and premiums can be adjusted as hospital and medical costs go up. Several major insurors issue policies that are guaranteed renewable but maintain the right to raise premiums.

Guaranteed renewable policies usually fall into one of three categories:

1. Renewable to age sixty-five with premiums and benefits ending then.

2. Renewable for life with premiums remaining the same, but with reduced benefits after age sixty-five.

3. Paid up at age sixty-five with premiums ending at that point, but with reduced benefits continuing for life.

Hospitalization policies are constantly changing. Companies tend to place more and more limitations on their plans as greater use (and, at times, abuse) is being made of them. They find it difficult to keep pace with the rising costs of medical care as well as their own company's administrative costs. Those that broaden benefits often charge generous premiums, sometimes bordering on the absurd.

Hospitalization certainly cannot be considered an essential segment of the physician's insurance program as long as he owns a good major medical plan. However, it can be a useful supplement under some circumstances.

55. *Special Policies*

Covering the Unusual

Are you a week-end pilot?

Do you like to play football in your spare time?

Do you travel constantly?

Do you always purchase flight insurance before boarding a plane? There are several special policies which may be of interest to you. They can serve as supplements to your insurance program in those areas in which you normally may not be covered. Here are some:

1. Accidental death benefits attached to a life insurance policy specifically exclude private flying. If you do pilot a plane, you may want to own a global pilot's accident policy. This covers you in the event of death or dismemberment while engaged in private aviation. It may be obtained by you for the benefit of your family or it may be purchased by your partner for the protection of his interests. Riders providing for disability income and medical reimbursement can be added. Premiums for this aviation coverage at any age are from about $59 a year for $10,000 of coverage to about $293 a year for $50,000.

2. Another global accident policy on the market covers accidental death or dismemberment except when caused by private flying. This, too, may be taken out by a business associate. Disability income and medical reimbursement riders can be added. Premiums at all ages run from about $23 a year for $15,000 to $150 a year for $100,000. If you fly scheduled airlines quite often, it may be less expensive to own one of these policies than to buy flight insurance each time you board a plane. Furthermore, it will afford protection between flights and all year.

3. The joint global accident policy covers two lives on one policy for accidental death and dismemberment, except under the condi-

tions of private aviation. This can be very useful to the partners who are constantly traveling. Premiums for coverage on both lives are from about $18 a year for $10,000 to $175 a year for $100,000.

4. Some companies issue an accident medical reimbursement policy. This pays all bills, including hospital, doctor, drugs, special equipment, relating to treatment for injuries. It is not a policy heavily advertised by insurance companies or agents because it is a "door opener," and represents little or no profit to either. For $500 indemnity, for example, the premium is only about $14 a year for boys, $12 a year for girls, $12 a year for a housewife, and $15 a year for a physician. This policy is especially suitable for covering small children who are most susceptible to minor accidents.

Various other unusual coverages are available. Even amateur stock car racers, volunteer firemen, and week-end sportsmen, can obtain policies to cover special risks.

Any physician who engages in unusually dangerous hobbies or sports should investigate these special plans.

56. *Taxes and Insurance*

Tax Questions and Answers Related to Insurance

Tax laws change constantly. Court decisions often clarify regulations which have never received a practical test.

Listed below are just a few of the many questions that are often raised in relation to insurance. In all instances, the answers shown are of a general nature and do not take into consideration exceptions, complications, variations, or new changes. Any specific questions relating to your particular circumstances should be discussed with your tax advisor.

FEDERAL INCOME TAX AND INSURANCE

Q: Are premiums paid for life insurance deductible?

A: No.

Q: Are premiums paid by a partnership, or a partner, for insurance on a copartner deductible?

A: No.

Q: Are premiums paid by a partner for insurance on his own life, naming a copartner as beneficiary, deductible?

A: No.

Q: Are premiums paid for insurance on the life of a divorced man with his former wife as beneficiary, considered taxable income to the wife and deductible by the husband?

A: If the policy, by court decree or written separation agreement, is absolutely assigned to the wife, premiums are deductible by the husband and constitute taxable income to the wife.

Q: Are life insurance premiums deductible if a charitable organization is named as irrevocable beneficiary?

A: Yes, if the insured also relinquishes the right to surrender the policy. The limits on charitable contribution deductions apply.

Q: Are life insurance premiums paid to benefit a creditor deductible by the debtor?

A: No.

Q: Are premiums paid for waiver of premium, accidental death, and disability income riders in a life insurance policy deductible as a medical expense?

A: No.

Q: Are benefits received under these riders taxable?

A: No.

Q: Are the proceeds of life insurance to a personal or business beneficiary exempt from income tax?

A: Yes.

Q: Are death proceeds of life insurance taxable if they are paid to a trust?

A: No. The trustee is considered the same as any other beneficiary. He may be a named beneficiary to receive money which he then disburses as per a trust instrument.

Q: Are life insurance dividends taxable?

A: No. They are considered a refund of unused premium.

Q: Is the interest received on dividend accumulations taxable?

A: Yes.

Q: Is interest paid on a loan against a policy deductible?

A: Yes, in the year it is actually paid.

Q: Are discounts received for prepayment of premiums considered taxable income?

A: No.

Q: Are premiums that have been waived because of disability considered taxable income?

A: No.

Q: Is the increase in the cash value of a policy taxable income?

A: No.

Q: Are premiums paid by an individual for personal accident and health insurance deductible as a medical expense?

A: The portion of the premium paid for medical, surgical, or hospital expense reimbursement may be considered as having been paid for medical care, when computing medical expense deductions. That portion of the premium paid for indemnity against loss of earnings, dismemberment, or accidental death is not deductible as a medical expense.

Q: Are benefits from personal accident and health policies taxable?
A: No.
Q: How is accident and health insurance, purchased by a partnership for a partner, treated for tax purposes?
A: Premiums are not deductible, and income received is not taxable.
Q: Are premiums on an office overhead policy deductible? Are the proceeds taxable?
A: This coverage is not considered personal accident and health insurance. Premiums are deductible and proceeds are taxable.

FEDERAL ESTATE TAX AND INSURANCE

Q: When are life insurance proceeds includible in the insured's gross estate?
A: When the estate is named beneficiary, when the insured at his death possessed incidents of ownership, and when he has transferred ownership of a policy within three years of his death.
Q: What constitutes incidents of ownership?
A: Power to change beneficiaries, to assign, surrender, or cancel the policy, to revoke an assignment, to pledge the policy for a loan, to borrow against it; each of these constitutes an incident of ownership.
Q: Can life insurance proceeds be arranged to qualify fully or partially for the marital deduction?
A: Yes.
Q: If a wife owns, and is beneficiary of, a policy on her husband's life, will the proceeds be includible in the husband's estate?
A: No, if he had no incidents of ownership.
Q: If an ex-husband is required to maintain life insurance in favor of his former wife, are the proceeds taxable in his estate?
A: No, if he has absolutely assigned the policy and retained no incidents of ownership.
Q: Are life insurance proceeds payable to charitable, educational, or religious institutions taxed?
A: No.
Q: If partners purchase life insurance on each other to fund a buy and sell agreement, are the proceeds of the insurance includible in the deceased's estate?
A: No, if the insured had no incidents of ownership in his policy and if the estate was not named beneficiary. The value of his partnership interest as fixed in the agreement, however, is includible.
Q: Are death benefits received under riders attached to accident and

health policies considered the same as life insurance proceeds for estate tax purposes?

A: Yes, they are subject to the same rules as life insurance proceeds.

Q: Are proceeds from the accidental death provision of a life insurance policy includible in the gross estate?

A: Yes, just as any other life insurance proceeds.

Q: Are proceeds from group or association death coverages includible in the gross estate?

A: Yes.

Index